American Sign Language Basics
for
Hearing Parents of Deaf Children

Jess Freeman King, Ed.D.
Jan Kelley-King, M.S.

Butte Publications, Inc.
Hillsboro, Oregon, U.S.A.

Editor: Ellen Todras
Reviewers: Sandy Harvey, Dr. McCay Vernon
Cover design: Anita Jones
Page design: Anita Jones
Illustrations: Anita Jones

Butte Publications, Inc.
P.O. Box 1328
Hillsboro, OR 97123-1328

ISBN 1-884362-06-0
Printed in U.S.A.

Dedication

To the many parents of deaf children who have
touched our lives and encouraged us
to write this book, and
to Laura Beth, Jess Benjamin, and Bethany Jane

Foreword

In following the careers of Freeman King and Jan Kelley-King over the years, I have developed great admiration for their contributions to linguistics and communication, particularly as those apply to the field of deafness. With publication of this book they have provided a clear, concise introduction to what is perhaps the most fascinating of all means of human communication, American Sign Language (ASL).

For mothers and fathers of deaf children, this book creates an opportunity to break the communication barrier deafness often creates between a parent and a deaf child. Ironically, until recent years ASL was a forbidden language, rejected by schools, denied to deaf children, and banned as "off limits" by educators. Only through the research of psycholinguists and the emergence of deaf people as leaders in education has ASL finally begun to assume the major role it should have in educating and parenting deaf children.

Unfortunately, until *American Sign Language Basics for Hearing Parents of Deaf Children* was made available, parents had no comprehensive program available for learning how to communicate with their deaf child. Previous texts and videos were either geared to learning to communicate with deaf adults, dealt only with specific subject areas, or were essentially dictionaries. By contrast, this book and video present an integrated program for mastering basic sign language. Presented in easy-to-master format, the book moves along at a comfortable pace that allows readers to become progressively more competent in American Sign Language. Short, clear chapters take the reader through the basic principles and grammar of ASL in easy, gradual steps which include practical lessons and activities parents can use in developing ASL competence.

By mastering the lessons this book provides, parents can develop the communication tools which will enable them to effect a close, emotional bond with their deaf child. In addition, this enhanced communication capability makes accessible to the child the social, educational, and psychological guidance and information parents who lack competence in sign language are often incapable of offering their deaf children.

McCay Vernon, Ph.D., Psychologist
Professor Emeritus, Western Maryland College
Consultant to Deaf Unit, Springfield Hospital Center

This book is long overdue! Twenty years ago, as a young mother, I remember searching for a book that would help my family learn to sign to our son. *American Sign Language Basics for Hearing Parents of Deaf Children* will guide parents as they learn the basics of American Sign Language in their own homes, in a comfortable and natural environment.

American Sign Language Basics for Hearing Parents of Deaf Children is not a dictionary. American Sign Language is made easy through the exercises and activities. The book offers lots of encouragement to parents as they discover a visual way to communicate. It is a pleasure for me to recommend this book to all new parents interested in communicating with their children who are Deaf or Hard of Hearing.

Sandy Harvey
Executive Director
American Society for Deaf Children

Table of Contents

Foreword..iv

Introduction...ix

    How to Use This Book..xi
    Glosses...xii

Unit 1 *Getting Started*

    Lesson 1 Identifying Family Members..3
    Lesson 2 Facial Expression..5

Unit 2 *Declarative Statements*

    Lesson 3 Declarative Statements: Like and Don't Like.............................9
    Lesson 4 Declarative Statements: Want and Don't Want........................13
    Lesson 5 Declarative Statements: Need and Must...................................17

Unit 3 *Questions*

    Lesson 6 Questions: Yes/No...23
    Lesson 7 Questions: Changing Statements into Questions......................27
    Lesson 8 Questions: Wh-..31

Unit 4 *Verbs*

    Lesson 9 Non-Directional Verbs...37
    Lesson 10 Directional Verbs...41

Unit 5 *Pronouns*

    Lesson 11 Indexing..47
    Lesson 12 Using Pronouns..51
    Lesson 13 Possessive Pronouns...55
    Lesson 14 Classifiers...59

Unit 6 *Timeline in ASL*

    Lesson 15 Past Tense...69
    Lesson 16 Future Tense...75
    Lesson 17 Temporal Aspect...79

Unit 7 *Word Order*

Lesson 18 Topic-Comment Principle...87
Lesson 19 Noun-Adjective Relationship.......................................91
Lesson 20 Three-Signs-or-Less Principle......................................95
Lesson 21 Time Indicators...99
Lesson 22 Time Sequence Principle...103

Unit 8 *Sign Modification*

Lesson 23 Showing Different Meanings by Altering Facial Expression and
Movement of the Sign...109
Lesson 24 Number Incorporation..113

Unit 9 *Other Topics*

Lesson 25 Plurality..121
Lesson 26 Showing Courtesy..127
Lesson 27 Conceptual Signing..131
Lesson 28 Fingerspelling...137

Appendix A: *Manual Alphabet*...141
Appendix B: *Numbers*...143
Appendix C: *Resources*..145

Introduction

It is important that you as a hearing parent, who happens to have a child who is deaf, realize that you can learn the basics of American Sign Language (ASL). With regular practice and interaction with users of this visual language, you can progress well beyond the basics. By learning the basic principles and grammatical structures involved in ASL and actively using them with your child, you will be opening up a world of communication accessibility and will be providing your child with a full, complete language that will make the English language even more accessible.

By following the principles and absorbing the grammatical structure hints and vocabulary that are presented in this text, you can learn basic American Sign Language. You will find that the study of ASL is a rewarding and fascinating adventure. Your success or failure with this language depends very much upon your attitude as you approach the subject.

It is natural to be anxious concerning your ability to learn ASL, but remember that if you are motivated and are willing to put in the time and effort and follow the guidelines presented in this book, you will learn American Sign Language. You will be opening up a magnitude of positive social, educational, and emotional opportunities for your child that otherwise will remain closed.

You are embarking on a venture that will provide a natural means of communication for your child. American Sign Language is a beautiful, visual language that is easily accessible and will daily reinforce the fact that having a child who is deaf can be a wonderfully exciting experience.

Your child, by virtue of being deaf, is naturally a visual learner and will blossom linguistically, socially, and emotionally by having an accessible visual language.

What is American Sign Language?

American Sign Language is the visual language that is used by the majority of Deaf adults in the United States and Canada. It is a complete language with its own structure, grammatical rules, and idiomatic expressions. ASL is a highly complex language, allowing the free and natural expression of any thoughts and concepts that might be produced in a spoken language.

As noted author and American Sign Language expert Lou Fant states, "The uniqueness of ASL lies in the simple fact that it is based upon light waves rather than sound waves. It is a visual, as opposed to an aural language. Meaning is conveyed by sight, not sound." Wouldn't a language that is based on vision rather than hearing logically lend itself to fulfilling the communication needs of the parent and the child who is deaf—the child who because of not being able to hear the English language spoken will depend on his/her vision and will naturally gravitate toward a language that is of a visual nature?

How does American Sign Language differ from English and manually coded English sign systems?

Both English and American Sign Language are complete languages, each possessing its own unique word/sign order and linguistically appropriate properties. The main difference between the two is that English is a spoken and a written language while American Sign Language is a visual-spatial language that does not have a written form (however, with the widespread use of videotapes, ASL might be considered to have a "written form").

Speech is only one manifestation of having acquired the English language. Do not be tempted to equate speech and language! If your child has the ability to learn to use speech, the learning and use of ASL will in no way be a detraction. In fact, having a strong language base (ASL) can enhance the development of a second language.

The arranging of signs in English word order is referred to as manually coded English and is an attempt to present English in a visual manner. Manually coded English is a linguistic system; American Sign Language is a true language that is easier learned by both the hearing parent and the child who is deaf. American Sign Language is not simply a matter of arranging ASL signs in English word order and speaking English at the same time. Becoming fluent in ASL involves learning and using some basic principles and by interacting with the Deaf community as much as possible.

Why should you learn basic American Sign Language?

There are a number of valid reasons why the hearing parent of a deaf child might want to learn basic American Sign Language and use it as the language for meaningful, open communication in the home. First of all, research has shown that ASL presents to the child a visual-motor feedback system that parallels the auditory-articulatory (hearing-speaking) system utilized by hearing children in their spoken language. In fact, some scholars feel that American Sign Language should be the primary language presented to all children who are deaf, regardless of the degree of hearing loss, because it more readily affords access to the school curriculum. Other researchers even go so far as to state that there is adequate theoretical support to promote the incorporation of ASL in a bilingual program as a tool to teach English literacy skills.

Your mastery of basic American Sign Language will also open up to you as a hearing parent contacts and interaction with the Deaf community. You will learn that Deaf people are in no form handicapped and that given an equal education and equal opportunities, a person who is deaf can do anything that a hearing person can do. Deaf people do not view their deafness as a handicap: the only handicapping possibility occurs when a complete, natural language is not provided at an early age.

By learning American Sign Language, you will be providing your child the opportunity to interact meaningfully with members of both the Deaf and hearing cultures. You will be communicating a message to your child that few children who are deaf have the opportunity to understand: it is alright to be Deaf, and he/she can do and can be anything that his/her heart desires.

However, the most valid reason for you as a hearing parent to learn American Sign Language is that it will provide an avenue for you to have meaningful and direct one-on-one communication with your child. You can learn ASL!

Suggestions for practicing and applying the ASL that you will learn

Learning American Sign Language is like learning any foreign language: you must practice the language and interact with it on a regular basis, preferably with native users of the language, in order to become proficient. Sorry, there are no shortcuts. However, by following and practicing the principles presented in this text, the ease with which you learn basic ASL will be greatly enhanced.

Try to separate yourself from English during your practice times. Even though you will be tempted to try to use speech and ASL at the same time, you will find this impossible to do, because the word/sign order of the two languages are vastly different. Trying to use them simultaneously will only confuse you and slow down your progress in learning ASL. Force yourself not to use your voice as you practice. Instead, concentrate on the visual aspects of American Sign Language, and your practice times will be much more beneficial.

It is important that you constantly give yourself positive feedback regarding your ability to master the basic principles of American Sign Language. As you invest more time and energy in practice, you will become more confident in your ability to use ASL.

In your study of American Sign Language, you will be learning the rules and grammar that govern the language. Just like English or other spoken languages, American Sign Language is a flexible language; that is, there are always exceptions to the rules. The only way to become skilled in the complete language of ASL is to interact with native users of the language, the adults in the Deaf community. The importance of this interaction cannot be stressed enough because it is the foundation that facilitates your becoming a truly skilled user of American Sign Language and knowledgeable about the culture of the American Deaf community.

Congratulations to you and best wishes as you venture forth into learning a new language that will ultimately pay great dividends for both you and your child. You are taking the first step toward providing your child with a way to have an open and exciting language ... an open and exciting means for communicating ... and an entrance into an exciting world which without this first step by you might very possibly never occur.

How to Use This Book

Each chapter of your text has been divided into three basic sections: 1) Some information introducing the concept that the lesson focuses on, 2) Practice, and 3) Activities. This logical breakdown will assist you in mastering the basic principles of American Sign Language.

The initial paragraphs of the lesson provide a basic explanation of the ASL concept presented in the chapter. You will often be provided with a comparison/contrast to a similar construct that occurs in the English language.

The Practice section leads you immediately into a parallel between the English language and American Sign Language. This section will enable you to instantly use your knowledge of the ASL concept presented in the chapter by constructing complete ASL sentences. Often sentences in the Practice section will be demonstrated on the videotape. In addition, all material that appears on the Practice videotape is identified by an icon in the margin of the text.

The Activities section provides you with games and activities that can be participated in by your child and other family members. Through this section you can begin interacting with your child via games and activities of a meaningful, hands-on nature that will enhance and facilitate linguistic growth.

There are also two other components that make up your complete package: 1) the portion of your text called Appendices, and 2) your videotapes.

The appendices of your text include illustrations of basic numbers and the manual alphabet, and a resources section to guide you to further study as you feel it useful.

Your two videotapes provide you with visual demonstrations of many of the practice sentences in the text as well as examples of various ASL concepts and structures from the book.

By utilizing your book and the accompanying videotapes, you will be on your way to becoming proficient in the basics of American Sign Language. Remember, however, how important it is that you become involved as much as possible with the adult Deaf community; it is through interaction with native users of ASL that you will become truly fluent.

Glosses: A Form of Translation

You will notice throughout your text that many ASL glosses are presented for you to practice. A gloss is the written ASL translation of an English sentence. By way of example, a word gloss might be explained by using a language with which you might be more familiar, Spanish.

Following is a sentence written in Spanish with an accompanying English gloss and translation:

> Spanish sentence:
> Le gusta a usted dulce?

> English gloss for the Spanish sentence:
> It like you candy?

> English translation of the Spanish sentence:
> Do you like candy?

Clearly, the gloss is not the correct way that the Spanish sentence would be spoken or written in English; it is only an approximation of a word-to-word comparison. The same holds true when writing an English gloss of an American Sign Language sentence.

Remember, you will never communicate by writing or speaking in English glosses for ASL, because it is impossible to incorporate the correct word order and intent of a visual language via speech or the printed word. American Sign Language is a visual language that is based on visual principles.

Therefore, the English glosses that occur throughout the book are only here to provide a hint as to the ASL sign order and how you should sign the sentence. Many aspects of ASL are very difficult to write in an English gloss. Therefore, you should pay particular attention to non-manual behaviors (facial expressions and body language) which are important parts of American Sign Language.

Unit 1

Getting Started

Lesson 1
Identifying Family Members

Deaf people within a group of friends often have name signs for one another. Instead of fingerspelling "Jennifer" every time someone wants to mention her, her name sign will be used. Sometimes name signs are given to a person based on a physical characteristic or personality trait.

For example, if "Mary" tends to smile a lot, her name sign may be made with the "M" hand shape using the same location and movement as the sign for smile. If "Carl" wears glasses, his name sign may be made with the "C" hand shape near the eye.

However, many name signs are arbitrary and have no reference to physical characteristics. An example may be a "J" on the shoulder for "John."

It is important to remember that name signs are normally known and used only among a certain group of friends and would not be recognized outside of that group. In other words, Mary, who teaches at the School for the Deaf, will probably have a different name sign than Mary who works at the bank. Coincidentally, someone you meet at an American Society for Deaf Children's conference may have the same name sign as Mary, but her name might be Margaret or Sara Mitchell.

It will be helpful to your child for you to come up with name signs for his/her friends and family members. This will make it easier to identify and refer to family and friends.

To identify a family member or friend in American Sign Language, it is okay to:
1) point first, then use the sign for the family member or friend,
2) use the sign first and then point to the family member or friend,
3) simply point to the family member or friend, or
4) use the sign only.

Lesson 2
Facial Expression

Facial expression is an important part of American Sign Language. It is a part of the grammar of ASL.

In English, we use punctuation or changes in our voices to indicate differences between questions and statements, to suggest pauses in conversation, or to show emotions such as anger, sadness, or surprise.

Because ASL is a visual language, not an auditory or written language, the grammatical markers happen on the face and body. These grammatical markers, called non-manual markers, are a crucial part of ASL. If you do not include facial expression, your signs will not have meaning. It would be similar to talking in a monotone or writing sentences with no punctuation.

As you are practicing, you will be given hints to help you remember what facial expressions to use in certain situations.

As you are using sign language with your child, use normal and natural facial expressions. Also, try to copy the facial expressions that are used on your videotape.

Practice and Activities

1. Just for fun, play facial expression games. During a meal or at other times when family members are together, do all of your communicating with facial expressions and gestures only (no voice or sign!). Your family will probably be surprised just how much can be communicated in this way.

2. Playing charades with an emphasis on facial expressions may help family members become more comfortable with using facial expressions.

3. Practice using facial expressions in front of a mirror with members of your family. You can play follow the leader with facial expressions, where everyone must copy the leader's expression. A large mirror makes it even more fun so that you can see yourself and others at the same time.

4. If you have a video recorder, you can record your family on video practicing different expressions and then watch the video together.

5. Focus on interesting, meaningful facial expressions along with your ASL signs for a period of time (portion of a day, a full day, a week, etc.). You may want to post reminders around your home or work place such as, "Be expressive!" or "Work on your expression!"

Unit 2

Declarative Statements

Combining facial expressions with some simple noun and verb signs can immediately start you on your way to communicating with your child in American Sign Language. With just a few basic combinations of signs, you will be surprised at how quickly communication will be established.

In this section you will work with the signs for LIKE, DON'T-LIKE, WANT, DON'T-WANT, NEED, AND HAVE-TO. When signing the positive terms, you should have a normal, natural, and pleasant look on your face, and nod your head slightly. When signing the negative terms, modify your facial expression appropriately and shake your head slightly.

You will want to learn some family signs (MOTHER, BROTHER, and so forth) to use with your practice sentences and activities.

To begin, it is important that you understand American Sign Language is a topic-comment language. That is, the topic of conversation is established first, then the comment concerning the topic is signed. This sequence holds true for both declarative statements and questions.

Lesson 3
Declarative Statements: Like and Don't Like

Using some basic principles of ASL, you can begin effective communication with your child with just a few basic combinations of words.

For example, start with two basic verbs:
LIKE and DON'T LIKE

When signing LIKE, you should have a natural, pleasant look on your face and nod your head slightly. When signing DON'T-LIKE, you should use an unpleasant facial expression and shake your head slightly.

LIKE   DON'T LIKE

Some additional vocabulary you will need to get started

Some other important words you need to know are "you" and "I." These signs are made by pointing with the index finger to yourself for I and to your child or other person for YOU. ME is signed the same way that I is signed.

Practice

Here's a great activity that should be a lot of fun for you and your family. Place some different kinds of food or drinks on the table or get pictures of some food and drinks. Point to different items and use the signs you have learned to say whether you like them/don't like them. Go ahead and have fun with outlandish facial expressions! Remember your child is primarily a visual learner.

Practice Sentences for You to Try

ENGLISH	GLOSS FOR ASL
I like_____.	(point to item) I* LIKE
I don't like_____.	(point to item) I* DON'T-LIKE
I like apples.	APPLES I* LIKE
Daddy likes milk.	MILK DADDY LIKE
You don't like cheese.	CHEESE YOU DON'T-LIKE
You like ice cream.	ICE CREAM YOU LIKE
Sister doesn't like potatoes.	POTATOES SISTER DON'T-LIKE
I like bananas.	BANANAS I* LIKE

*It is not always necessary to use the sign for "I" when signing I LIKE. Your child and you may sign COOKIE LIKE or APPLE DON'T-LIKE and that is fine.

Activities

If you do not know the sign for a certain item, you can still practice these activities by just pointing to the item instead of using the name. Pointing to the item and then signing DON'T-LIKE is similar in English to saying "I don't like that." Have fun with the following activities.

1. Meal times and snack times are excellent times to practice expressing likes and dislikes in ASL with your child.

ENGLISH	GLOSS FOR ASL	
I like milk.	MILK I* LIKE	*I is optional
I like sandwiches.	SANDWICH LIKE	
You like ice cream.	ICE CREAM YOU LIKE	
I don't like potatoes.	POTATOES DON'T LIKE	
You like crackers.	CRACKERS YOU LIKE	

2. Children may have strong food preferences. You might want to look at what's in the refrigerator or go to the grocery store with your child and discuss what he or she likes or doesn't like.

ENGLISH	GLOSS FOR ASL	
I like carrots.	CARROTS I* LIKE	*I is optional
I don't like spinach.	SPINACH I* DON'T-LIKE	
You like chicken.	CHICKEN YOU LIKE	
You don't like bacon.	BACON YOU DON'T-LIKE	
You like cereal.	CEREAL YOU LIKE	
You don't like coffee.	COFFEE YOU DON'T-LIKE	

3. Go through magazines or catalogs with your child. Point out things that both of you like or don't like.

ENGLISH	GLOSS FOR ASL	
You like bicycles.	BICYCLES YOU LIKE	
You like cars.	CARS YOU LIKE	
I like shoes.	SHOES I* LIKE	*I is optional
You like pie.	PIE YOU LIKE	
I like the teddy bear.	TEDDY BEAR LIKE	

11

4. With some of the previous activities, it is a good idea to deliberately place things in front of your child that you know he or she does not like. Mix them with items your child does like. You can then practice the difference between like and don't like.

ENGLISH	GLOSS FOR ASL	
You like oatmeal.	OATMEAL YOU LIKE	
You like toast.	TOAST YOU LIKE	
You don't like eggs.	EGGS YOU DON'T-LIKE	
I like pancakes.	PANCAKES I* LIKE	*I is optional
You don't like coffee.	COFFEE YOU DON'T-LIKE	

5. Remember to give your child opportunities to express his or her likes and dislikes throughout the day by commenting on a particular activity, toy, book, or article of clothing.

ENGLISH	GLOSS FOR ASL	
I don't like to walk.	WALK DON'T-LIKE	
I don't like shoes.	SHOES DON'T-LIKE	
I like the dress.	DRESS LIKE	
I like the book.	BOOK I* LIKE	*I is optional

Lesson 4
Declarative Statements: Want and Don't Want

Now you can expand your use of declarative sentences by helping your child discuss what he/she wants or doesn't want.

I WANT

I DON'T-WANT

The sign for WANT is pulled toward you with palms up. Use a natural facial expression when using the sign WANT.

The sign DON'T-WANT is made by twisting the WANT sign away from your body. You should shake your head slightly when using the DON'T-WANT sign.

WANT   DON'T WANT

Practice

Using foods, toys, or photos is a good way to practice expressing wants. Roll up your sleeves, put on your dynamic facial expressions. Let's practice!

Practice Sentences for You to Try

ENGLISH	GLOSS FOR ASL
I don't want a banana.	BANANA I DON'T-WANT
I don't want any eggs.	EGGS DON'T-WANT
I want a cookie.	COOKIE WANT
Daddy doesn't want any sugar.	SUGAR DADDY DON'T-WANT
I want that book.	BOOK (point) WANT
I want some catsup.	CATSUP I WANT
I don't want any butter.	BUTTER DON'T-WANT ME
Sister wants some milk.	MILK SISTER WANT
Mom doesn't want onions.	ONIONS MOM DON'T-WANT
You don't want cheese.	CHEESE YOU DON'T-WANT
You don't want any more.	MORE DON'T-WANT YOU

(Remember, "I" is optional.)

Activities

The same activities that you used to practice like and don't-like can be used to practice want and don't want. You may also want to try the following:

1. From time to time put things a little out of the way (out of reach) so that your child will need to ask for them. For example, put the crackers on a high shelf or your child's favorite toy out of reach. Make a game out of this. Soon you will be searching for items that little Pedro has hidden from you!

ENGLISH	GLOSS FOR ASL
I want a cracker.	CRACKER I WANT
I want some cookies.	COOKIES I WANT
I want the ball.	BALL I WANT

2. Give your child a small amount so that he/she will need to ask for more. For example, pour just a little juice in the cup instead of filling it, or give him/her just a tiny piece of cake instead of a large one. Don't get carried away and become sadistic with this activity!

ENGLISH	GLOSS FOR ASL
I want cake.	CAKE WANT
I want juice.	JUICE WANT
I want more.	MORE
I want more.	WANT MORE
I want more milk.	MORE MILK WANT
I want more cereal.	CEREAL MORE WANT

3. Put several toys or objects in front of your child. When he/she shows a preference for one or more of the objects (points to or reaches for it), immediately reinforce him/her by signing.

EXAMPLE: Your child reaches for the doll.	
YOU SIGN: You want the doll.	DOLL YOU WANT
You want the ball.	BALL YOU WANT
You want the truck.	TRUCK YOU WANT

4. Help your child identify what he/she wants by playing with another family member. Let a brother, sister or Dad sit with your child and indicate in ASL what object he/she wants. Then respond by giving him/her the object. This could be a super activity for the entire family.

> EXAMPLES:
> SISTER: DOLL I WANT
> YOU: DOLL YOU WANT (then give the doll to Sister)
> BROTHER: BALL I WANT
> YOU: BALL YOU WANT (then give the ball to Brother)
> DADDY: APPLE I WANT
> YOU: APPLE YOU WANT (give Daddy an apple)
> DADDY: BOOK I WANT
> YOU: BOOK YOU WANT (give Daddy the book)

5. On some occasions you may want to deliberately offer your child something you know he/she doesn't want or offer something additional to eat when you think your child is probably full, just to create opportunities for practice. Sounds evil, doesn't it? But this is a fine activity for practicing don't-want.

ENGLISH	GLOSS FOR ASL
You don't want peas.	PEAS YOU DON'T-WANT
You don't want more.	MORE DON'T-WANT
You don't want any bread.	BREAD YOU DON'T-WANT

Lesson 5
Declarative Statements:
Need and Must

Now expand your sentences a little more with the following statements:

I NEED
I DON'T NEED
YOU DON'T HAVE TO (MUST)

The concepts "need, must, should, and have-to" are expressed by using the same sign. You can use the sign as a statement of a fact such as, "I need some more milk," or you can be more forceful with it: "You have to go to bed."

NEED/MUST

DON'T
(then add the NEED sign)

Just as you would hear the difference between those two statements in speech, your youngster will see the difference in your facial expression and stress placed on the sign. Cue your videotape and see the difference in facial expression and movement.

The concepts "don't need" and "don't have to" are expressed by adding a negative to the sign NEED. This is accomplished by using the sign NOT, by shaking the head, or doing both, and then signing NEED. If you're confused by the verbiage, consult your videotape.

Hint: The sign NEED tends to come after the verb or noun.

Practice
Practice Sentences for You to Try

ENGLISH	GLOSS FOR ASL
📼 I need some more milk.	MILK MORE NEED
	-*or*- MORE MILK NEED
📼 You don't have to eat your bread.	YOU BREAD EAT NOT NEED
📼 We don't need any cheese.	WE* CHEESE NOT NEED
📼 You need to take a bath.	BATH YOU NEED
📼 I don't need a jacket.	JACKET I* NOT NEED
I need some more money.	MORE MONEY I* NEED
Sister must go to school.	SISTER SCHOOL GO MUST
I need to use the rest room.	I* BATHROOM MUST
You should share.	YOU SHARE MUST
I don't have to work.	WORK NOT NEED

(* I/we is optional)

More Practice Sentences for You to Try

ENGLISH	GLOSS FOR ASL
I want an apple.	APPLE WANT (ME)
I don't want a banana.	BANANA DON'T-WANT
You like to play.	PLAY YOU LIKE
You should share.	SHARE MUST YOU
You need to stop playing.	PLAY STOP MUST YOU
Sister doesn't want to swing.	SWING SISTER DON'T-WANT
	-*or*- SISTER DON'T-WANT SWING
I like books.	BOOK ME LIKE
You need to go to bed.	YOU BED/SLEEP NEED
You need to go to sleep.	YOU BED/SLEEP NEED
You need to go to your bedroom.	YOU BEDROOM GO NEED
I need to cook.	COOK MUST ME
You must get dressed.	YOU GET-DRESSED MUST
You need to brush your teeth.	YOU BRUSH-TEETH MUST
Daddy needs some more milk.	MORE MILK DADDY NEEDS
	-*or*- DADDY MORE MILK NEED
You want another cookie.	MORE COOKIE YOU WANT
You need to go to the bathroom.	BATHROOM YOU NEED
You like to run.	YOU RUN LIKE

Putting It All T-o-g-e-t-h-e-r

Practice using combinations of words to make some basic statements in ASL. Choose any word from column one and follow it with any word in column two.

You can also add YOU or I or a family member at the beginning by using the sign for the person or pointing to yourself or anyone in the room.

sit	need, must, have-to, should
go	like
eat	want
play	don't-like
swing	don't-want
read	
share	
stop	
cook	
clean	
more	
juice	
cookie	
book	
milk	
banana	
apple	
ball	
truck	
bathroom	
brush teeth	
get dressed	
go to bed	
rest	
wake up	

Activities

1. The same activities that were used for expressing I WANT or I LIKE can be used for expressing I NEED. Put things just out of reach of your child so he/she must ask for them. Fill up your child's glass with only a little milk or juice so that he/she can practice telling you what is needed or wanted.

2. Let your child help you with some daily routines such as setting the table, washing clothes, or picking up toys.

    EXAMPLE:
    You are setting the table and leave out something obvious like plates or forks. Show your child the place setting, then sign:

We need forks.	FORKS NEED
We need plates.	PLATES NEED

3. Plan an activity with your child that he/she is used to, such as coloring or taking a bath. Omit something that will be obvious to your child such as crayons, paper, soap, etc.

    EXAMPLES:
    You prepare for your child's bath. He/she is in the tub and you sign SOAP NEED. Sit down with crayons and no paper. Then sign PAPER NEED.

4. During daily activities there are always things that you, family members, or your child must do. Use these opportunities to practice using the sign HAVE-TO, MUST.

ENGLISH	GLOSS FOR ASL
Daddy has to go to work.	DADDY WORK GO MUST
You have to brush your teeth.	YOU BRUSH TEETH MUST
I have to cook.	I COOK MUST
You must stop playing.	YOU PLAY STOP MUST

Unit 3

Questions

In spoken English, questions are distinguished from statements by the order in which the words are arranged in a sentence and by the inflection in the voice. In the written form of English, question marks occur at the end of the sentence to distinguish between a question and a statement.

American Sign Language also distinguishes between questions and statements. However, in ASL the grammatical markers that indicate whether or not a sentence is a question are of a visual nature, not auditory as in the spoken language. These visual markers occur on the face and the body and are extremely important in differentiating between a statement and a question.

You recently learned how to combine basic signs into ASL sign order to form declarative sentences: how to state whether you like or don't like; want or don't want; and if you need or have to do something. You can change basic declarative statements into questions simply by altering your facial expression and body movement.

Even though there are several types of question forms in American Sign Language, we are only going to focus on two of the most practical for you at the moment: basically, questions that require a yes or no response, and those that require other responses.

Lesson 6
Questions: Yes/No

You can use the signs and sentences that you have already learned and easily change them into questions by changing your facial expression. When you want to ask a question that requires a yes or no response, you should lean forward a little with your eyes widened and your eyebrows up or arched. You also hold the last sign a little longer. By the way, the last sign is usually the question word.

For example, in English we say, "Do you want to play?" In ASL, the question part ("Do you want to") is typically signed after the topic, action, or object you are referring to.

You can begin by first putting two signs together, such as PLAY and WANT, to ask a question such as, "Do you want to play?"

The reminder in parenthesis (Q-y/n) is to help you remember to lean forward a little with your eyebrows arched because you are asking a question that requires a yes or no response.

EXAMPLES:

ENGLISH	GLOSS FOR ASL
Do you want to play?	PLAY WANT (Q-y/n)
Do you like ice cream?	ICE CREAM LIKE (Q-y/n)
Do you need a drink?	DRINK NEED (Q-y/n)

Encourage YES or NO responses from your child.

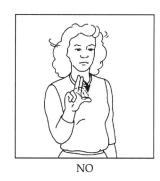

YES   NO

23

Practice

REMEMBER that in each of the following examples the question part (do you?) happens on the face with your eyebrows arched and head forward: (Q-y/n)

Practice Sentences for You to Try

ENGLISH	GLOSS FOR ASL
Do you want to play?	PLAY WANT (Q-y/n)
Do you like ice cream?	ICE CREAM LIKE (Q-y/n)
Are you finished eating?	EAT FINISH YOU (Q-y/n)
Does Daddy want to play?	DADDY PLAY WANT (Q-y/n)
Do you need to go to the bathroom?	BATHROOM NEED YOU (Q-y/n)
Do you need a drink?	DRINK NEED (Q-y / n)
Do you want to go to the store?	STORE YOU GO WANT (Q-y/n)
Do you like to go to school?	SCHOOL GO YOU LIKE (Q-y/n)
Do you want some milk?	MILK YOU WANT (Q-y/n)
Do you want to go outside?	GO OUTSIDE WANT (Q-y/n)
Do you need a tissue?	TISSUE YOU NEED (Q-y/n)
Do you need help?	HELP-YOU NEED (Q-y/n)
Do you like dogs?	DOGS YOU LIKE (Q-y/n)

Activities

1. At snack time, bring out several items your child might like, such as fruit, crackers, or cookies. Ask your child what he or she wants.

ENGLISH	GLOSS FOR ASL
Do you want an apple?	APPLE YOU WANT (Q-y/n)
Do you want a cracker?	CRACKER YOU WANT (Q-y/n)
Do you like cookies?	COOKIE YOU LIKE (Q-y/n)

2. In preparation for a meal, you may want to take your child to the pantry or the shelves where food items are stored and ask your child what he/she wants.

ENGLISH	GLOSS FOR ASL
Do you want peas?	PEAS YOU WANT (Q-y/n)
Do you want corn?	CORN YOU WANT (Q-y/n)

3. Dressing time is also a good time to ask yes/no questions. Ask your child about each item of clothing.

ENGLISH	GLOSS FOR ASL
Do you like the shoes?	SHOE (point) YOU LIKE (Q-y/n)
Do you need a coat?	COAT NEED (Q-y/n)
Do you want this shirt?	SHIRT (point) YOU WANT (Q-y/n)

4. Playtime is a great time to ask yes/no questions. You can ask your child what he/she wants to play with.

ENGLISH	GLOSS FOR ASL
Do you want the doll?	DOLL YOU WANT (Q-y/n)
Do you want the blocks?	BLOCKS YOU WANT (Q-y/n)
Do you want to swing?	SWING YOU WANT (Q-y/n)

5. To help your child respond to the yes/no questions, you can deliberately offer the child a toy or food item that he or she did not ask for. Here we go again! The impish side of you gets to play!

EXAMPLE:
Child points to his ball.
You offer the puzzle and ask YOU WANT (Q-y/n)
Your child may shake his head no until you offer the right item.
You can sign THIS (point) YOU DON'T-WANT for each item your child
doesn't seem interested in.

6. When selecting a book for story time, select a book and ask your child if he/she likes that one or wants that one.

<u>ENGLISH</u>

Do you like this book?

Do you want this book?

<u>GLOSS FOR ASL</u>

BOOK (point) YOU LIKE (Q-y/n)

BOOK (point) YOU WANT (Q-y/n)

Lesson 7
Questions:
Changing Statements into Questions

Now you can use all of the signs that you know to make statements and to change these statements into questions that have a yes or no response. The only change you need to make is in your facial expression. For statements, just have a normal, natural facial expression, as you would when speaking. For questions, change to the (Q-y/n) facial expression by arching your eyebrows and moving your head slightly forward.

EXAMPLES:

ENGLISH	GLOSS FOR ASL
You want to read.	YOU READ WANT
Do you want to read?	YOU READ WANT (Q-y/n)
Daddy likes milk.	MILK DADDY LIKES
Does Daddy like milk?	MILK DADDY LIKE (Q-y/n)

27

Practice

Practice Making Statements and Questions (Q-y/n)

With the words below, practice using different combinations to make sentences. First use them to ask questions, then change them into statements.

play	like
work	don't like
eat	want
swing	don't want
read	need or need to
cookie	
books	
milk	

Practice Sentences for You to Try

ENGLISH	GLOSS FOR ASL
I want to read.	ME READ WANT
Do you want to read?	YOU READ WANT (Q-y/n)
Daddy likes milk.	MILK DADDY LIKES
	-or- DADDY LIKES MILK
Do you like milk?	MILK YOU LIKE (Q-y/n)
	-or- YOU LIKE MILK (Q-y/n)
Sister doesn't like to swing.	SWING SISTER DON'T-LIKE
	-or- SISTER SWING DON'T-LIKE
Do you like to swing?	SWING YOU LIKE (Q-y/n)
	-or- YOU LIKE SWING (Q-y/n)
I want the ball.	ME BALL WANT
Do you want the ball?	YOU BALL WANT (Q-y/n)
	-or- YOU WANT BALL (Q-y/n)
Grandpa needs help.	GRANDPA HELP NEED
Does Grandpa need help?	GRANDPA HELP NEED (Q-y/n)
Mom likes flowers.	FLOWERS MOM LIKE
Does Mom want some flowers?	FLOWERS MOM WANT (Q-y/n)
Sister wants some milk.	MILK SISTER WANT
Does Sister want some milk?	MILK SISTER WANT (Q-y/n)
You should go to the bathroom now.	NOW BATHROOM GO MUST YOU
Do you have to go to the bathroom now?	NOW BATHROOM GO MUST YOU (Q-y/n)
We have to eat now.	NOW EAT MUST
Do you want to eat now?	NOW YOU EAT WANT (Q-y/n)

28

More Practice Sentences

Now, using a combination of just a few words, see how many different sentences you can express in ASL by changing a few grammatical markers (facial and body movements). Choose one word from each column to make a statement and then change it into a question.

Remember to use an affirmative head nod for "like" and "want" and shake your head for "don't want" and "don't like."

brother	want	cookies
sister	don't-want	play
mom	like	read
dad	don't-like	flowers
grandma	must, have-to	orange juice
I, me	need	help
you	should	drink
grandpa		go

Activities

1. As often as you can when you sign a question, answer it by changing the question into a statement. Remember to use appropriate facial expressions with your questions.

BOOK YOU WANT?	(arch eyebrows, head slightly forward)	BOOK YOU WANT
COOKIE YOU WANT?	(arch eyebrows, head slightly forward)	COOKIE YOU WANT
SWING YOU WANT?	(arch eyebrows, head slightly forward)	SWING YOU WANT
BATHROOM YOU NEED?	(arch eyebrows, head slightly forward)	BATHROOM YOU NEED

2. At mealtime, you may want to emphasize the changing of questions into statements.

EXAMPLES:
You sign: POTATOES YOU WANT?
(child indicates "yes")
You sign: POTATOES YOU WANT
You sign: BACON YOU WANT?
(child indicates "no")
You sign: BACON YOU DON'T-WANT

3. You can use the same question and statement activity described in #2 during playtime with different toys. Involve other family members in the activity as well. Remember, the whole family, friends, and school personnel should be involved. You are striving for a total and consistent visual language experience.

EXAMPLES:
Mom asks sister: DOLL YOU WANT (Q-y/n)
Sister answers: NO
Mom replies: DOLL YOU DON'T WANT

Mom asks sister: BALL YOU WANT (Q-y/n)
Sister answers: YES
Mom replies: BALL YOU WANT
(Don't forget to give her the ball!)

Lesson 8
Questions: Wh-

You learned earlier that there are basically two types of questions in ASL. One type requires a yes or no response. You learned how changing your facial expression and body movement can change a statement into a question.

The other type of question is one that requires an answer other than a yes or no response. In English these questions begin with words such as who, what, what happened, when, where, why, which, and how. For ease of reference, we will call these "wh-" questions.

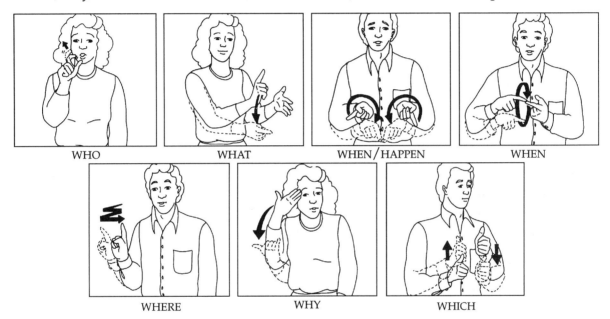

WHO   WHAT   WHEN / HAPPEN   WHEN

WHERE   WHY   WHICH

In ASL, these question words/signs typically come at the end of a sentence. The facial expression and body movements are different than with yes/no questions. For these "wh-" questions, the head tilts to the side and the eyebrows are furrowed. The hint (Q-wh) in the examples is to help you remember which facial expression to use.

Sometimes the signs for a statement, a "yes/no" question, or a "wh-" question will be the same. Only your facial expression and body movement indicate that you are asking or stating different things.

EXAMPLE:

ENGLISH	GLOSS FOR ASL
You have many children.	CHILDREN MANY HAVE YOU
Do you have many children?	CHILDREN MANY HAVE (Q-y/n)
How many children do you have?	CHILDREN MANY HAVE (Q-wh)

The only difference occurs on the face and body, not on the hands. That is why facial expressions are sometimes referred to as non-manual grammatical markers. Although there is a separate sign for HOW, you would not have to use it with the sign MANY as long as you include the (Q-wh) facial expression.

31

Practice

Practice Sentences for You to Try

ENGLISH	GLOSS FOR ASL
▣ What time will the movie start?	MOVIE BEGIN TIME (Q-wh)
▣ Why is your jacket dirty?	YOUR JACKET DIRTY WHY (Q-wh)
▣ Do you want milk or water?	YOU WANT MILK WATER WHICH (Q-wh)
▣ Where is your sister?	SISTER YOUR WHERE (Q-wh)
▣ How do you feel?	HOW YOU FEEL (Q-wh)
Where is Daddy?	DADDY WHERE (Q-wh)
Who is that man?	MAN THERE WHO (Q-wh)
What is in the box?	BOX IN WHAT (Q-wh)
Why are you crying?	YOU CRY WHY (Q-wh)
Do you want to stay or leave?	YOU WANT STAY LEAVE WHICH (Q-wh)
How did you get wet?	YOU WET HOW ((Q-wh)
	-or- YOU WET HAPPEN (Q-wh) (means what happened?)
What time does school start?	SCHOOL BEGIN TIME (Q-wh)
Which book do you want?	BOOK-YOU-WANT-WHICH (Q-wh)
Do you want an apple or banana?	YOU WANT APPLE BANANA WHICH (Q-wh)

More Practice Sentences

Comparing Yes/No and Wh- Questions
HINT: If you change the expression to (Q-y/n) you will change the question.

ENGLISH	GLOSS FOR ASL
▣ Is he old?	HE (point) OLD (Q-y/n)
▣ How old is he?	HE (point) OLD (Q-wh)
▣ Do you have many children?	CHILDREN MANY HAVE (Q-y/n)
▣ How many children do you have?	CHILDREN MANY HAVE (Q-wh)
▣ Is your house far away?	YOUR HOUSE FAR (Q-y/n)
▣ How far away is your house?	YOUR HOUSE HOW-FAR (Q-wh)

Activities

Remember to use the (Q-wh) facial expression.

1. Put some things in a box or sack for your child to find. Ask your child:

ENGLISH	GLOSS FOR ASL
What is in the box?	BOX IN WHAT (Q-wh)
	-or - BOX WHAT IN (Q-wh)
Where is the ball?	BALL WHERE (Q-wh)
	-or- WHERE BALL (Q-wh)
Is the ball in the box?	BALL IN BOX (Q-y/n)

2. Sit down with your child and ask him/her to locate some familiar things in the house. For example, sit in the living room and ask your child to locate things in that room.

ENGLISH	GLOSS FOR ASL
Where is Daddy?	DADDY WHERE (Q-wh)
Where is the remote control?	TV REMOTE WHERE (Q-wh)
Where is the family picture?	FAMILY PICTURE WHERE (Q-wh)

3. Go through a family photo album and ask your child to identify the people by pointing to the person in the picture that you ask about.

ENGLISH	GLOSS FOR ASL
Where is Mommy?	MOMMY WHERE (Q-wh)
Where is Brother?	BROTHER WHERE (Q-wh)

Use the same idea to practice "who." Point to someone in the picture and ask your child:

ENGLISH	GLOSS FOR ASL
Who is that man?	MAN THERE (point) WHO (Q-wh)
Who is that girl?	GIRL THERE (point) WHO (Q-wh)

4. Practice using the "wh-" expression during the day.

ENGLISH	GLOSS FOR ASL
Who broke the chair?	CHAIR BROKE WHO (Q-wh)
Why is the baby crying?	BABY CRY WHY (Q-wh)
What happened?	WHAT HAPPENED (Q-wh)

(With the right facial expression, you do not have to sign WHAT.)

5. You can use "wh-" questions when watching TV with your child or reading a story. Ask your child questions about what is happening.

ENGLISH	GLOSS FOR ASL
Where is the girl's mother?	GIRL MOTHER WHERE (Q-wh)
People are laughing. What happened?	PEOPLE LAUGH HAPPEN (Q-wh)
Why did the wolf blow down the house?	WOLF BLOW HOUSE-DOWN WHY (Q-wh)
Why was papa bear mad?	PAPA BEAR MAD WHY -or- HAPPEN (Q-wh)

6. Practice using the "wh-" facial expression with the sign for making choices: WHICH. Put several favorite toys in front of your child and ask him/her to make a choice.

ENGLISH	GLOSS FOR ASL
Do you want the ball or the truck?	BALL TRUCK YOU WANT WHICH (Q-wh)
Do you want the book or the doll?	BOOK DOLL YOU WANT WHICH (Q-wh)

7. At snack times, ask your child to make choices for a snack.

ENGLISH	GLOSS FOR ASL
Do you want juice or milk?	YOU WANT JUICE MILK WHICH (Q-wh)
Do you want a cracker or an apple?	YOU WANT CRACKER APPLE WHICH (Q-wh)

Remember to tilt your head to the side and furrow your brow.

Unit 4

Verbs

American Sign Language has several distinctions of verbs. For the purposes of this text we will discuss only two categories:

1. non-directional verbs
2. directional verbs.

You will learn that with some verbs the direction of the movement is not changed and subjects and objects must be established with separate signs in order to show who is doing and receiving the action.

With other verbs, the direction of the movement of the verb itself can be modified to show who is doing and receiving the action.

Lesson 9
Non-Directional Verbs

Most verbs in American Sign Language require that you use a separate sign to indicate who is doing or receiving the action.

DADDY WORK   MOMMY COOK   SISTER EAT

These types of verbs are called non-directional verbs. You have already been using many non-directional verbs.

EXAMPLES:

play	eat
work	need
swing	stop
cook	drink
want	run
brush teeth	share
sit	
like	

Practice

Practice Sentences for You to Try

ENGLISH	GLOSS FOR ASL
Mommy is cooking.	MOTHER COOK
Brother has to study.	BROTHER STUDY MUST
Stop running.	RUN STOP
You brush your teeth.	YOU BRUSH-TEETH
You and your brother are sharing.	YOU BROTHER SHARE
Daddy is working.	DADDY WORK
You like to play.	YOU PLAY LIKE
Sister is swinging.	SISTER SWING

Activities

1. Try to notice the action going on nearby your child, and comment on it using the appropriate verbs.

   EXAMPLE:
   The man is running.   MAN (index) RUN

2. Keep an eye out for pictures from magazines that show a lot of action. Action pictures are great to keep in a scrapbook and look at with your child. You can combine every thing you have learned so far to talk about the pictures, using facial expressions, non-directional verbs, and asking questions. You can ask your child such questions as, "What are they doing?" or "What is happening?" Then you can help your child answer your questions by modeling the verbs to describe the picture.

   Action pictures are good for practicing facial expression while describing what is going on.

Lesson 10
Directional Verbs

With some verbs, the meaning of the action changes when the direction of the movement is changed. With directional verbs, the direction of movement is modified to show who is doing and receiving the action.

EXAMPLES:
give
borrow
show
loan
teach
help
meet
call

These verb signs move from the giver to the receiver. So if you wanted to say, "You give me the ball," you would sign BALL then move the GIVE sign toward you.

BALL YOU-GIVE-ME (the hyphens mean this is one sign, not three)

If you wanted to say, "I will give you the ball," you would sign BALL then move the GIVE sign from you out to the person you are talking to.

BALL I-GIVE-YOU

The signs can move in any direction to any person, depending on who is giving and who is receiving. Confused? No problem! Take a look at the example of directional verb usage in your videotape and all will be clear.

ENGLISH	GLOSS FOR ASL
Give me the ball.	BALL YOU-GIVE-ME (the sign GIVE moves from your child toward yourself)
I will give you the ball.	BALL I-GIVE-YOU (the sign GIVE moves from yourself toward your child)
You give Daddy the ball.	BALL YOU-GIVE-DADDY (the sign GIVE moves from the child toward Daddy)

41

Practice

Practice Sentences for You to Try

ENGLISH	GLOSS FOR ASL
� Show me the picture.	PICTURE YOU-SHOW-ME (Sign PICTURE, then move SHOW from child to yourself.)
▦ Help me clean up.	YOU-HELP-ME CLEAN (Move HELP from child to yourself, then sign CLEAN.)
▦ Give me the shoes.	GIVE-ME SHOES *-or-* SHOES YOU-GIVE-ME (Sign SHOES, then move GIVE from child to yourself.)
▦ I will help you get dressed.	YOU GET-DRESSED ME-HELP-YOU *-or-* ME-HELP-YOU GET-DRESSED (Sign GET-DRESSED, then move HELP from yourself to child.)
▦ Daddy will help you take a bath.	DADDY HELP-YOU BATHE *-or-* YOU BATHE DADDY HELP-YOU
Help Daddy.	YOU HELP DADDY *-or-* DADDY YOU-HELP-HIM (Sign DADDY, point to him, sign YOU, then move HELP from child to Daddy.)

Activities

1. Play a game with your child with a few favorite toys. Put some toys or familiar objects within reach of your child. You can start by either pointing to an object or using the sign for the object and then signing GIVE-ME. Let your child respond first by giving you the object. Then you respond by giving the object back.

   YOU: BALL YOU-GIVE-ME (child gives you the ball)
   CHILD: BALL YOU-GIVE-ME (give the ball back)

   If your child does not ask for the ball, you can respond:

   YOU: BALL ME-GIVE-YOU (then give the ball back)

   Then you can put the toys in your reach only and let your child start the game.

2. Play the same game above with another family member so that the sentence can be shown to the child. Daddy may ask for a toy and Mom can give it to Daddy; then it is Sister's turn. Now your child can see what is expected.

	ENGLISH	GLOSS FOR ASL
DADDY:	Give me the car.	CAR YOU-GIVE-ME
MOM:	I'll give you the car.	CAR I-GIVE-YOU (Mom gives him the car)
SISTER:	You give me the doll.	DOLL YOU-GIVE-ME
MOM:	I will give you the doll.	DOLL I-GIVE-YOU (Mom gives her the doll)

3. Let your child help you with different tasks around the house such as washing, cooking, cleaning, working outside, etc. Tell your child as you are working, YOU-HELP-ME.

ENGLISH	GLOSS FOR ASL
You help Daddy work.	DADDY WORK YOU-HELP-HIM
You help me cook.	YOU-HELP-ME COOK

4. Notice when your child is having difficulty with something such as a package he or she can't open, something that is out of reach, or a door that won't open.

   Use these opportunities to sign ME-HELP-YOU.

5. You can have another family member pretend to have difficulty with something and ask the child for help.

   Sign YOU-HELP-ME.

6. Hide something in a bag or behind your back and tell your child or other family member that you will show him or her what it is.

     ME-SHOW-YOU

Let your child hide something and you ask him or her to show you what it is.

     YOU-SHOW-ME

7. Look for opportunities when your child is playing alone, possibly coloring a picture or making something. You can use that opportunity to ask your child to show you what he/she is doing.

ENGLISH	GLOSS FOR ASL
Show me the picture.	PICTURE YOU-SHOW-ME
Show me the book.	BOOK YOU-SHOW-ME

Unit 5

Pronouns

The use of space around the body when signing is an important part of ASL. Space is used to refer to people, places, and things, as well as to different time periods and events. Often a topic will be signed and followed by indexing (pointing to a specific space near the body). From that point on in a conversation or story, that topic can be referred to by pointing back to that specific space.

In the English language pronouns are used quite often instead of repeatedly using their referents. For example, we use words such as *he* or *she* instead of saying the person's name over and over again. ASL uses pronouns too. In ASL pronouns can be shown through spatialization and indexing. Spatialization means using the index finger to point to a specific area in space after using the sign for the referent (noun). Indexing is used once the referent is assigned a specific space. This means the signer can refer back to that space by again using the index finger to point to that space. First-person pronouns such as *I, he, she, they,* and *it* as well as third-person pronouns such as *me, him, her,* and *them* are shown by indexing.

Possessive pronouns are shown by referring to the specific area in space, using the open palm handshape (be sure to keep the fingers together).

Another way pronouns can be used in ASL is through the use of classifiers. Classifiers are handshapes that represent certain types of nouns, and the action associated with the noun.

Lesson 11
Indexing

Indexing or pointing to people and places in space is used quite often in ASL, in the same way that English uses words such as *this, that, there*, and *here*.

INDEX

In English we say things like:
Bring me that book.
Put the dishes over there.
This cup is broken.
There is my teacher.

ASL uses indexing for the same purpose.
BOOK (point) GIVE-ME
DISHES PUT (point)
CUP (point) BROKEN
MY TEACHER (point)

Practice

Practice Sentences for You to Try

ENGLISH	GLOSS FOR ASL
Give me those socks.	SOCKS (point) YOU-GIVE-ME
I don't like those shoes.	SHOES (point) I DON'T-LIKE
I want that book.	BOOK (point) I WANT
That picture is pretty.	PICTURE (point) PRETTY
That shirt is dirty.	SHIRT (point) DIRTY
You need to pick up these toys.	TOYS (point) YOU PICK-UP NEED
Put your jacket over there.	JACKET PUT (point)
Help me move this.	THIS (point) YOU-HELP-ME MOVE
I like that dress.	DRESS (point) I LIKE

Activities

* When you see the words HERE and THERE written for the gloss you should point to the item being referred to.

1. Involve your child in picking up toys, clothes, and other items around the house. Sign the items and then point to where they go.

ENGLISH	GLOSS FOR ASL
There are the shoes.	SHOES THERE
The doll goes there.	DOLL THERE
There is the shirt.	SHIRT THERE
The blanket goes there.	BLANKET THERE

2. Let your child help you put dishes away. Slave labor or teaching responsibility? You're doing great! Keep it up.

ENGLISH	GLOSS FOR ASL
The cup goes here.	CUP HERE
The spoon goes there.	SPOON THERE
The fork goes there.	FORK THERE
The bowl goes there.	BOWL THERE

3. Let your child help you fold and separate clothes.

ENGLISH	GLOSS FOR ASL
Here are Brother's socks. Brother's socks go here.	BROTHER SOCKS HERE
Here are the kitchen towels. Kitchen towels go here.	KITCHEN TOWELS HERE
Here are the bathroom towels. Bathroom towels go here.	BATHROOM TOWELS HERE
There are the shirts. Shirts go here.	SHIRTS THERE

4. Go for a ride or a walk with your child and discuss what you see.

ENGLISH	GLOSS FOR ASL
There is a duck swimming.	DUCK THERE SWIM
There are dogs running.	DOGS THERE RUN
The man there is tall.	MAN THERE TALL
The colors of those trees is pretty.	TREES THERE COLORS PRETTY
There is a big truck.	TRUCK THERE BIG

5. Throughout the day, refer to persons or places that are present by describing them and pointing.

ENGLISH	GLOSS FOR ASL
Your sister is crying.	SISTER (point) CRY
Daddy is washing dishes.	DADDY (point) DISHES WASH
Brother is riding a bike.	BROTHER (point) RIDE-BIKE
The baby is asleep in his room.	BABY SLEEP IN ROOM (point)

6. When giving instructions to your child, use references to persons or places.

ENGLISH	GLOSS FOR ASL
You play outside.	YOU PLAY OUTSIDE (point)
Get down.	GET DOWN (sign YOU then point down)
Come here.	COME HERE (YOU COME point)
Go downstairs.	YOU GO DOWNSTAIRS (point)
Tell Daddy to come here.	TELL DADDY (point) COME HERE (point)

Lesson 12
Using Pronouns

In ASL, pronouns (he, she, they, me, you, them, him, her, it) are indicated by indexing (pointing to the actual person or thing with your index finger or giving that person or thing a designated place in space and referring back to it by pointing).

HIM/HE/SHE/HER/IT/THAT   THEY/THOSE/THEM   I/ME   YOU

Suppose you were in a group talking about a friend named Jim who was not there. In English you would not say, for example: "Where is Jim?" "Oh, Jim had to work." "What time does Jim get off?" "Jim works until 8:00 tonight." "Let's call Jim tonight." Instead, you would use the word *he* or *him* in place of Jim's name after you had established to whom you were referring.

When using ASL for a similar conversation, you would not continue to fingerspell Jim's name every time Jim was mentioned. Instead, the first time you mentioned Jim's name you would index or point (with the index finger) to a particular area in space either to the right or left. From that time on, each time Jim was referred to, you would simply point to that same area in space. This is called indexing and it is used just like pronouns are used in English.

If the person, animal, or object you wish to refer to is in sight, you simply point to him, her, or it.

For the pronouns ME and I, you should point with the index finger to yourself. For the pronoun YOU, simply point to the person you are addressing. For the pronouns HE, HIM, HER, OR SHE, you index (point to) the person to whom you are referring.

For more than one person, place, or thing (the use of pronouns such as THEY, THEM, THOSE), a sweeping motion (left to right) with either the index finger or an open hand with palm facing up may be used. If more than one person, place, animal or object is talked about, you should index different areas of space around the body for each one. Don't be confused, just consult your video. You're making progress!

Practice

Practice with Pronouns

In the examples below, when you see the word (index) next to a word, it means you should point to a space either to your right, left, or in front of you. When you see, for example, a pronoun written "HE (index)" the only thing you need to do is point to a particular place.

For indexing the pronouns THEY, THEM, and THOSE, sometimes an open hand with palm facing up is used in a sweeping motion instead of the index finger.

If more than one person, animal, or object is talked about, remember to use different areas in space for each one.

Practice Sentences for You to Try

ENGLISH	GLOSS FOR ASL
He wants to play.	HE (index) PLAY WANT
You and I are friends.	YOU ME FRIENDS
Give the book to her.	BOOK YOU-GIVE-HER (index)
She helped me clean up.	SHE (index) HELP-ME CLEAN
Daddy is in bed. He is sick.	DADDY BED HE (index) SICK
Does he (father) want to go?	FATHER (index) GO WANT (Q-y/n)
Mom can't go.	MOM (index right) GO CAN'T
Dad can't go.	DAD (index left) GO CAN'T
Can you go?	YOU (index) GO CAN (Q-y/n)
He threw the ball and she caught it.	HE (index right) BALL THROW SHE (index left) CATCH
He smiled.	HE (index right) SMILED
He gave me the juice.	JUICE HE (index) GIVE-ME
The remote control is over there.	REMOTE THERE (index)
Jim is in his room. He can't play.	JIM IN ROOM HE (index) PLAY CAN'T

Activities

1. Playing with dolls or plastic animals is a good way to emphasize pronouns. Name the doll or sign the animal name and use the pronoun for it by pointing.

ENGLISH	GLOSS FOR ASL
The cow is brown.	COW (index) BROWN
It has two friends.	COW (index) FRIENDS TWO HAVE (point to each cow)
They eat grass.	THEY (point to each cow) EAT GRASS
The baby doll is cute.	DOLL BABY CUTE
She has a mom and a dad.	SHE (index) MOM DAD HAVE
She has one brother.	SHE (index) BROTHER ONE HAVE (point to him)
He likes to ride bikes.	HE (index) RIDE-BIKE LIKE
She likes to jump rope.	SHE (index) JUMP-ROPE LIKE
The horse can run fast.	HORSE RUN FAST CAN
It is strong.	HORSE (index) STRONG
It eats a lot.	HORSE (index) EAT MUCH

2. Look through your family album. Find pictures of family members and comment on what they are doing in the picture. Use pronouns (indexing) to discuss what they are doing.

ENGLISH	GLOSS FOR ASL
Grandma has a pretty dress.	GRANDMA DRESS PRETTY HAVE
She will come visit.	SHE (index) COME VISIT WILL
She loves you.	SHE (index) LOVE YOU
Daddy looks silly.	DADDY LOOK/FACE SILLY
He is working.	HE (index) WORK
He likes to play with you.	HE (index) PLAY WITH YOU LIKE

3. As you are discussing other family members with your child, remember to use pronouns where appropriate.

<u>ENGLISH</u>

Daddy is working outside.
He looks tired.

Brother is playing over there.
He is playing.

Jim and Ben fight. That isn't nice!
They are fighting.
That isn't nice.

<u>GLOSS FOR ASL</u>

DADDY WORK OUTSIDE
HE (index) LOOK TIRED

BROTHER PLAY (point to an area)
HE (index) PLAY

JIM BEN FIGHT NOT NICE
THEY (point to each) FIGHT
NOT NICE

Lesson 13
Possessive Pronouns

In ASL possession is usually shown with the open palm/hand. Extend the open palm facing the person or designated area in space to represent possessive pronouns (HIS, HERS, THEIRS, YOURS, MINE).

HIS/HERS/THEIR/YOUR   THEIRS/YOURS   MINE   OUR

For the possessive pronoun MY or MINE, place or tap the open palm on your chest.

For the possessive pronoun YOUR, move the open palm toward the person you are addressing.

For the possessive pronouns HERS and HIS, simply move the open palm in the direction of the person to whom you are referring; if the person is not present, assign him/her a place in space by indexing.

For the possessive pronoun THEIRS, you would move the open palm in a sweeping motion toward the group to which you are referring.

The exception to the open palm rule is the possessive pronoun OUR. OUR is made by tracing a half-circle with the right hand from the right side of your chest to the left side. The curved palm faces the chest and moves from right shoulder to left shoulder. (If you are left-handed, start the movement on your left shoulder.) See the illustration and video.

Be careful to use the open palm for the pronouns YOURS, MINE, HIS, HERS, and THEIRS and to use the index finger for the pronouns YOU, ME, HER, HIM, SHE, HE, and THEY. If you forget, may your videotape knot into a thousand kinks!

Practice

Practice Sentences for You to Try

ENGLISH	GLOSS FOR ASL
This book is mine.	BOOK (index) MINE
Where is yours?	YOUR BOOK WHERE (Q-wh)
	-or- BOOK YOUR WHERE (Q-wh)
Her picture is pretty.	GIRL (index) HER (open palm) PICTURE PRETTY
His teacher is nice.	BOY (index) HIS (open palm) TEACHER NICE
My aunt is coming to visit.	AUNT MINE COME VISIT
My family loves to ski.	FAMILY MY SKI LOVE
My father is sick.	MY FATHER (index) SICK
He can't come visit.	HE (index) VISIT CAN'T
Can I see your horse?	HORSE YOUR ME SEE CAN (Q-y/n)
Their dog is missing.	DOG THEIRS (open palm) GONE

Activities

1. Children like to have ownership of things. They like to be able to say, "This is mine." Play a game with your child by getting some things together that belong specifically to him/her and some other things that belong to you or other family members.

   You can put the things in a bag or box and pull one out at a time and discuss whose they are.

   EXAMPLE: You could sign sentences such as:

ENGLISH	GLOSS FOR ASL
This is my wallet.	WALLET MINE
This is your car.	·CAR YOUR
This is her doll.	DOLL HER
That book is his.	BOOK HIS

2. Folding and putting away clothes is a good time to involve your child in practicing possessives. Have a separate stack for each family member's clothing. Point to things that are yours and sign MINE. Point to things that are your child's and sign YOURS. Let your child have a turn as he/she picks up items of clothing.

3. You can also use possessives to ask questions. You can point to different items in the house and ask your child:

ENGLISH	GLOSS FOR ASL
Is it yours?	YOURS (Q-y/n)
Is it mine?	MINE (Q-y/n)

   Remember, (Q-y/n) means to lean forward a little with your eyebrows arched, and for (Q-wh) to furrow the eyebrows and have a questioning look.

Lesson 14
Classifiers

Classifiers are handshapes that are used to represent people, places, or things, and certain groups or classes of items. They are often used in ASL to represent, to describe, or to show action easily and efficiently.

Below are some classifiers and the kinds of things they can be used to represent. These are demonstrated for you on the first videotape.

	HANDSHAPE	WHAT IT REPRESENTS
	CL: 1	one person
	CL: 2	two people walking together legs walking eyes looking around
	CL: CROOKED 2 *or* CL: CROOKED 3	person sitting animal chair
	CL: 3	any land or water vehicle three people walking
	CL: F	flat round objects such as coins or buttons thin cylindrical object such as a ski pole eyes looking around
	CL: C	thick cylindrical object like a tree trunk (two hands) cups or cans (one hand)
	CL: MODIFIED C (like the letter)	larger flat round objects like plates (two hands) stack of things such as papers (one hand) can be used to show the thickness of a book (one hand)

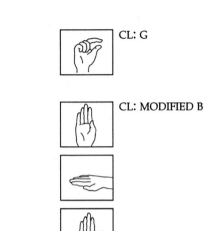

CL: G   narrow border like a picture frame
something thin like a small stack of papers or a layer
of dust

CL: MODIFIED B   flat surface like a shelf or table
also used to show contour of the land such as a ski
slope, hills, or flat terrain

CL: 5 CLAW   clumps of trees
buildings
groups of things

Remember that facial expression is very important when using classifiers too. Watch how your videotape presenter changes his or her facial expression and the movement of the classifier to show different meanings.

Practice

We have many colorful verbs and adverbs in the English language. These can easily be described in ASL by changing the movement of verbs or the classifiers themselves. Some of the following examples are shown on the first videotape. Watch the examples and then try them and some of the others on your own.

EXAMPLES:
a big man walking heavily
a thin lady walking lightly
a bear lumbering along
a mouse scampering
a rabbit hopping along
a car speeding by
a big log truck struggling up a hill
a motorcycle zooming between cars
a sailboat gracefully riding the waves

Practice Sentences for You to Try

ENGLISH	GLOSS FOR ASL
The girl walked along happily.	GIRL HAPPY (CL:1 moves with a quick bouncy movement)
Your shirt has red buttons.	SHIRT YOUR RED (CL:F moves down front of shirt) HAVE
The boat sank.	BOAT (CL:3 moves downward slowly in a sinking motion)
The cat chased the mouse.	CAT (place CL: CROOKED 3 left hand in front of you) MOUSE (place CL:3 CROOKED 3 right hand in front of left hand) (Move the two hands forward showing the left hand chasing the right hand)
There are clumps of trees on the hilly landscape.	(CL: B palm down moves in a wavy motion showing the rolling hills) TREE (CL: CROOKED 5 is moved from place to place along the slope to show where the trees are)

Practice Stories

The first practice story is shown on the instructional videotape, not the practices videotape.

A boy was walking along (CL:1 left hand moves forward) when he saw a girl (CL:1 right hand is placed in front of left hand). He looked at her (CL:2 left hand palm down faces right hand CL:1), their eyes met (CL:2 right hand palm down faces CL:2 left hand palm down), and he was taken by her (facial expression/body shift). He approached her (both hands go back to CL:1 position left hand moving toward right hand), but she turned away (right hand CL:1 moves away). The boy became saddened. (Facial expression/body shift)

I was driving my car very slowly (right hand CL:3 shows that movement)) when a car pulled up behind me and started following me right on my bumper (left hand CL: 3 shows that movement). The other car kept moving over into the left lane to try to pass me (left hand CL: 3 shows that movement). Finally I slowed and moved over to the right (right hand CL: 3 shows that movement), and the car went flying by me (left hand CL: 3 shows that movement).

Activities

1. Use some dolls or toys that your child likes to play with. Show the doll walking fast. Then show the action with CL: 1. Next, show the doll walking slowly. Then show that action with CL: 1.

2. You can describe similar actions with a toy animal, by using CL: CROOKED 2. You can make the animals chase each other, run, walk, jump, etc. using classifiers.

3. You can use some toy cars to show the use of CL: 3. You can use both hands and show the cars passing each other or one bumping into another. Describe the action with the toy cars and then show the action with the classifiers, CL: 3.

4. Look at pictures in a magazine. Point out items that could be described using classifiers. Refer back to the list of classifiers.

   EXAMPLES:
flagpole (small)	CL:F
flagpole (large)	CL:C
dishes	CL: MODIFIED C
animals	CL: 2 CROOKED
person	CL:1
coins	CL:F
slide	CL:B
person looking up at the sky	CL:2

5. Describe action that takes place when you are with your child. Use classifiers to describe that action.

   EXAMPLES:
Car back out of parking place at the store.	CL: 3
You see two people walking together.	CL: 2
You see horses running.	CL: 2 (CROOKED)

Unit 6

Timeline in ASL

ASL has an imaginary timeline that runs through the signer's body. What does this mean? Signs for the past tense occur behind the head and body on this line. Signs for future tense occur in front of the head and body on this line. Think about whether the signs are referring to past tense or future tense, and pay attention to where they occur in relation to the head and body.

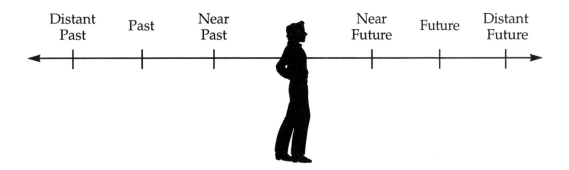

Present tense occurs in line with the head and body.

NOW
>   Both hands side by side "Y" position, palms up in front of the body.

IMMEDIATELY
>   Use the NOW sign but bring it closer to the body and make it more intense.

DAY
>   The left arm is placed palm down in front of body. The right hand is in a "1" position. The right arm with elbow resting on the left fingers moves downward until arms are touching.

DAILY/EVERYDAY
>   Right hand in "A" position, palm touching cheek moves forward across the cheek several times. The wrist is kept straight with the palm always facing left.

TODAY
>   Combine the signs NOW and DAY.

WEEK
>   Left hand in front of body, palm up. Right index finger moves across the palm.

THIS WEEK
>   Combine the signs NOW and WEEK.

WEEKLY/EVERY WEEK
>   The sign for WEEK is repeated.

MONTH
>   The left index finger is held up, palm facing to the right. The right index finger palm facing you, finger pointing to the left, starts at the top of the left finger and slides down to the second joint.

THIS MONTH
>   Combine the signs NOW and MONTH.

MONTHLY
>   The sign for MONTH is repeated.

YEAR
>   With palms facing you, the right hand "S" position moves forward and around the left "S" coming to rest on top of the left "S."

THIS YEAR
>   Combine the signs NOW and YEAR.

YEARLY / ANNUALLY / EVERY YEAR
>   Repeat the sign for NEXT YEAR (see next page).

Future tense signs move in front of the head and body.

TOMORROW
> Right hand in the "A" position, thumb touching cheek moves forward and out from the face, the wrist twisting the thumb up.

FUTURE
> The right hand in a "5" position with fingers together starts at the side of the head and moves forward (entire arm moves forward).

A SHORT TIME FROM NOW (little bit into the future)
> Use the FUTURE sign but move it just a little bit past the cheek.

A LONG TIME FROM NOW (way into the future)
> Use the FUTURE sign but move it way out in front of the head.

NEXT WEEK
> Left hand in front of body, palm up. Right index finger moves across the palm and swings in a semicircle out in front of the body.

NEXT YEAR
> Place the right fist on top of the left fist, right palm facing left, left palm facing right. Then move the right hand up and forward into a "1" position.

Past tense signs occur or move behind the head and body.

YESTERDAY
Touch the right cheek with the thumb of either the "Y" position or "A" position and move the hand backward toward the ear.

2 DAYS AGO
The right hand "K" position is placed on the right cheek with palm facing behind you, middle finger touching cheek. Twist the wrist so that the palm is reversed with the palm facing in front of you and the index finger touching the cheek.

RECENTLY
The right hand "X" position touches the right cheek and moves back and forth slightly. Or the number "11" can be made with the right index finger at the cheek pointing back toward the ear.

PAST / AGO
The hand (fingers together and thumb extended) is held near the face with palm facing behind you, and moved in one motion behind you.

-or-

The hand (fingers together and thumb extended) is held near the face with palm facing in front of you. The entire arm makes a circling motion while moving behind the head.

A SHORT TIME AGO (little while into the past)
Use the first sign for PAST, but do not move the hand very far back.

A LONG TIME AGO
Use the second sign for PAST, making a larger circling motion back behind the head.

LAST WEEK
Left hand in front of body palm up. Right index finger moves across the palm and swings in a semicircle backwards.

LAST YEAR
Place the right fist on the thumb side (on top of) the left fist. Then move the right hand up and backward into a "1" position.

Lesson 15
Past Tense

Certain signs are used to indicate that something happened in the past.

    LONG AGO

    LAST YEAR, YESTERDAY, LAST WEEK, etc.

    FINISH

    IN THE PAST/BEFORE

Using Time Indicators to Show Past Tense

If your sentence starts with a time indicator that shows past tense, then the tense of the verb is known in that way.

EXAMPLES:

ENGLISH	GLOSS FOR ASL
We went to the zoo last week.	LAST WEEK ZOO GO

You know the verb must be past tense because the time indicator told you it happened last week.

ENGLISH	GLOSS FOR ASL
I ate fish yesterday.	YESTERDAY FISH EAT

You know the verb is past tense because of the time indicator YESTERDAY.

ENGLISH	GLOSS FOR ASL
I used to teach.	IN-THE-PAST ME TEACH

You know it is past tense because the IN-THE-PAST sign was used at the beginning of the sentence.

ENGLISH	GLOSS FOR ASL
I did not like school before.	IN-THE-PAST SCHOOL NOT-LIKE ME

It is easy to see that the verb is past tense because of IN-THE-PAST/BEFORE being used at the beginning of the sentence.

69

"Finish" as a Past Tense Indicator

Often, the FINISH sign will be used to show past tense. Most of the time, it will come after the verb.

EXAMPLES:

ENGLISH	GLOSS FOR ASL
I have eaten. I already ate.	ME EAT FINISH
Have you eaten?	YOU EAT FINISH (Q-y/n)
I went to the store.	STORE GO ME FINISH
I gave you the book.	BOOK GIVE YOU FINISH

FINISH

Practice
Practice Sentences for You to Try

ENGLISH	GLOSS FOR ASL
Grandpa was a soldier in the war.	LONG AGO WAR GRANDPA SOLDIER
Mom was sick.	PAST (short time ago) MOM SICK
I gave you 3 cookies.	COOKIE 3 GIVE-YOU FINISH
	-or- COOKIE 3 FINISH GIVE-YOU
You saw that movie.	MOVIE SEE FINISH YOU
Daddy used to live here.	PAST (long time ago) DADDY LIVE HERE
Brother broke the chair.	CHAIR BROTHER BROKE
	(context shows past tense)
Mom was angry this morning.	NOW MORNING MOM ANGRY
Mom isn't angry anymore.	MOM ANGRY FINISH
You just ate.	RECENT YOU EAT FINISH

Activities

1. When you finish an activity with your child, take a moment to discuss that activity using past tense indicators. For example, you and your child may bake cookies together. During the activity you can point out things you have already done using the FINISH sign.

EXAMPLES:	
ENGLISH	GLOSS FOR ASL
The eggs broke.	EGGS BREAK FINISH
We filled the sugar bowl.	SUGAR POUR-IN FINISH
We are done stirring.	STIR FINISH
We have turned on the oven.	OVEN TURN-ON FINISH

When the activity is completed, you can use past tense indicators to refer to that activity throughout the day.

EXAMPLES:	
ENGLISH	GLOSS FOR ASL
We baked cookies.	YOU ME COOKIES BAKE FINISH
We just made some cookies.	YOU ME RECENT COOKIES BAKE
We made cookies before.	PAST YOU ME COOKIES BAKE
We made cookies this morning.	NOW MORNING YOU ME COOKIES BAKE
We made cookies yesterday.	YESTERDAY YOU ME COOKIES BAKE

2. Keep a scrapbook of special activities, events, and places you visit. Include pictures, mementos, or souvenirs that you know your child will connect with that activity. From time to time get out the scrapbook and when talking about the contents, try to begin your sentences with the time indicator showing when the activity took place.

EXAMPLES:	
ENGLISH	GLOSS FOR ASL
Last year your birthday party was at McDonalds.	LAST YEAR YOUR BIRTHDAY PARTY MCDONALDS
You rode a horse.	(short time in the past) YOU HORSE RIDE
Last week you and Sister visited Grandma.	LAST WEEK YOU SISTER VISIT GRANDMA
Yesterday you and I found some pretty leaves.	YESTERDAY YOU ME LEAVES PRETTY FIND
Two weeks ago you and Daddy went fishing.	2 WEEKS AGO YOU DADDY FISHING

3. Look at a photo album with your child. Be sure the album has pictures that represent a long time ago, a short time ago, and the present. A baby book may be a good source. Use the PAST sign and modify it to show "way in the past" or "a short time in the past" to indicate when the picture was taken. For example:

GLOSS FOR ASL

LONG LONG AGO YOU BORN

LONG AGO YOU BIRTHDAY PARTY AGE 4

RECENT YOU VISIT Z-O-O

4. Show your child pictures of yourself or older members of your family when they were young. Use the LONG LONG AGO sign to describe the picture. You may use the signs for CHILD and GROW to indicate you grew up long ago.

Lesson 16
Future Tense

Future tense in ASL is shown through the use of specific signs that accompany the verb or begin the sentence.

Using Time Indicators to Show Future Tense

EXAMPLES:

ENGLISH	GLOSS FOR ASL
I have to work tomorrow.	TOMORROW ME WORK MUST
We will go to Grandma's next week.	NEXT WEEK GRANDMA HOUSE GO WILL
Next year you will be four years old.	NEXT YEAR YOU AGE-4 WILL
I will help you later.	LATER ME-HELP-YOU
The meeting will be tonight at 8:00.	NOW NIGHT TIME-8 MEETING

* SPECIAL NOTE: When WILL is used to mean intention to do something, it normally comes at the end of the sentence.

Practice
Practice Sentences for You to Try

ENGLISH

When you are big you will go to school.

Grandpa will come next week.

Next year you will go to school just like Sister.

A long time from now you will be as big as Daddy.

You will be staying with Grandma in two weeks.

You must go to the dentist tomorrow.

Your puppy will grow soon.

GLOSS FOR ASL

HAPPEN YOU BIG (indicate height) SCHOOL GO WILL

-*or*- GO SCHOOL WILL

NEXT WEEK GRANDPA COME WILL

NEXT YEAR YOU GO SCHOOL SAME SISTER

FUTURE (long time from now) YOU BIG (indicate height) SAME DADDY

TWO WEEKS FUTURE YOU STAY WITH GRANDMA WILL

TOMORROW DENTIST GO YOU MUST

FUTURE (short time from now) PUPPY WILL GROW

Activities

1. Before taking your child to a special place discuss with him/her where you will be going and when. When possible, plan such outings far enough in advance so that you can mark them on a calendar and use some future tense time indicators in your discussions.

    EXAMPLES:

ENGLISH	GLOSS FOR ASL
Next Saturday we will go to the zoo.	NEXT-WEEK SATURDAY WE GO ZOO WILL
Two days from now we will go to the zoo.	2 DAYS FUTURE WE GO ZOO WILL
Tomorrow we will go to the zoo.	TOMORROW WE GO ZOO WILL

2. When your child wakes up in the morning, you can discuss plans for the day using the future sign for intention to do something.

    EXAMPLES:

ENGLISH	GLOSS FOR ASL
Today Daddy will wash the car.	TODAY DADDY WASH CAR WILL
Will you help Daddy?	YOU HELP DADDY WILL (Q-y/n)
This afternoon you and I will go to the grocery store.	NOW AFTERNOON YOU ME GO FOOD STORE WILL
Tonight the family will watch a movie.	NOW-NIGHT FAMILY WATCH MOVIE WILL

3. You can make a distinction between the signs SHORT TIME FROM NOW and LONG TIME FROM NOW when your child asks for something that you can't quite help him with immediately. It may be something you can give him soon or it may be something you cannot help him with for a long time. Though he may not understand the concepts of time yet, you can respond with the appropriate signs.

    EXAMPLES:

CHILD: ME GO SCHOOL? (Q-y/n)
PARENT: NO CAN'T/YOU SMALL (indicate height, palm down)/FUTURE (long time from now) YOU BIG (indicate taller height, palm down) SCHOOL GO CAN

CHILD: COOKIE WANT!
PARENT: NO CAN'T/FUTURE (short time from now) COOKIE GIVE-YOU WILL

CHILD: SEE GRANDMA? (Q-y/n)
PARENT: NOT NOW (shake head while signing now)/TOMORROW SEE GRANDMA WILL

4. If your child has older siblings and younger siblings, you can use them to demonstrate some of the time-related signs. Use the CHILD sign to indicate differing heights of children in yourfamily.

> NOW YOU CHILD (show height of your child)
> SHORT-TIME-IN-FUTURE YOU CHILD (show little taller height) SAME BROTHER
> LONG-INTO-FUTURE YOU CHILD (show much taller height) SAME DADDY

Lesson 17
Temporal Aspect

You learned earlier how meanings of words can change if you change the movement of the sign or your facial expression.

The temporal aspect of ASL refers to showing how much time is involved in a particular activity or action. One way to do this is to state how much time was involved by signing concepts such as A LONG TIME, A SHORT TIME, ONE HOUR, A FEW MINUTES, AGAIN AND AGAIN, etc.

With some verbs, however, you can show the duration of time by altering the movement of the sign itself. Altering the sign in this manner is a great way to introduce the concept of "a long time" or "a short time" in a clear, visual manner.

View your videotape and all of this jargon will become clear to you. Remember that facial expression is important to practice with these signs. Watch the examples on the videotape and try to copy them.

EXAMPLES: (shown on the first videotape)

WAIT (SHORT TIME) - "Wait for me."
The sign is held in one place with fingers wiggling quickly.

WAIT (LONG TIME) - "I have been waiting a long time!"
The hands are moved in a circular motion moving out in front of the body while fingers wiggle steadily.

SICK - "I am sick."
The sign for SICK is made by touching the forehead with the middle finger of the right hand and the stomach with the middle finger of the left hand, or if you're a lefty, vice-versa.

SICK (CONTINUALLY OR REPEATEDLY) - "She is always sick."
The sign for SICK as described above is repeated with arms moving in a circular motion toward the body.

SIT - "May I sit here?"
The right curved index and middle fingers are placed crosswise on the left index and middle fingers (both palms down) in one movement.

SIT (FOR A LONG TIME) - "I sat and sat."
The sign for SIT is made as described above, but once the right fingers touch the left fingers they are held in that position while the hands circle out away from the body in a continuous motion.

79

LIE (TO LIE DOWN AND REST) - "Lie here and wait."
The left hand is placed in front of the body, palm up. The right hand with a "V" position (palm up) is placed on the left hand (palm up).

LIE DOWN (FOR A LONG TIME) - "I lay down for a long time."
The sign for LIE is made as described above but the right hand remains resting on the left palm while the hands circle repeatedly.

WATCH OR LOOK AT SOMETHING - "Look at the bird."
The "V" handshape is used, palm down, pointing toward what is to be viewed.

STARE AT SOMETHING OR TO WATCH FOR A LONG TIME - "The little girl stared and stared at the bird."
The "V" handshape, palm down, is used pointing toward the object being looked at, but the arm moves in a slight circular motion indicating it is happening for a long period of time.

LAUGH - "Did he laugh?"
Both hands, fingers together, are placed at the corners of the mouth and moved upward several times.

LAUGH (A LOT) - "Yes, he laughed a lot."
Use the sign for LAUGH as described above, but repeat the movement several times with a larger movement.

WASH - "I washed the dishes."
Rub one "A" hand repeatedly against the other "A" hand (palms facing).

WASH (A LOT) - "I washed many dishes."
Continue rubbing the hands together in a slow, repeated movement.

HURT - "I have a headache."
The index fingers are twisted in toward each other. This sign can be made specific to the area hurt: headache, tummy ache, etc.

HURT CONTINUALLY - "My head has been hurting for a long time."
Use the sign for HURT near the area of pain, such as head or stomach, and repeat the sign with a steady motion. The movement can also be modified by using a quick, sharp movement indicating a sharp pain.

ASK A QUESTION - "He asked a question."
The QUESTION sign with the index finger moves toward the person being asked. The question sign may occur at the beginning or the end of a sentence and is used with the appropriate facial expressions.

ASK A QUESTION AGAIN AND AGAIN - "She asked many questions."
The QUESTION sign moves toward the person being asked. This is done repeatedly to show asking more than one time. This sign can be made with both hands showing many questions being asked. The question sign is also a multi-directional verb sign. That is, it can be used to indicate who is asking the question of whom. Your videotape will clear up the confusion.

EAT - "I have to eat now."
The modified "O" position moves toward the mouth a few times.

EAT AND EAT AND EAT AND EAT - "The little boy eats a lot!"
You can repeat the sign for EAT using just one hand, or for more emphasis, use two hands and alternatively move your hands (modified "O" position) in circular movements toward your mouth.

WORK- "I must go to work."
The left "S" hand is placed palm down in front of the body. The right "S" position, palm forward, should strike the left wrist several times.

WORK HARD CONTINUALLY - "Mother works very hard."
Use the sign for WORK but repeat it and make the movement larger.

PLAY - "Children like to play."
Both "Y" hands, palms facing, are shaken several times in front of the body.

PLAY (FOR A LONG TIME) - "They played and played."
The sign for PLAY is extended and the movement exaggerated.

RAIN - "Do you like rain?"
The two curved "5" hands, palms down, bounce up and down a few times in front of the body (the movement is at the wrist).

RAIN (STEADY AND CONTINUOUS) - "Yesterday it rained and rained."
Make the sign for RAIN slow and continuous, moving the sign up and down with large arm movements. This sign can also be modified to show a hard downpour.

STUDY - "I need to study tonight."
The left hand is placed in front of the body with the palm facing you. The right "5" hand fingers, pointing toward the left palm, are then wiggled up and down.

STUDY FOR A LONG TIME - "I studied for a long time."
While making the sign for STUDY, both hands are moved in a circular motion.

STAND - "Stand near the tree."
The left hand is placed palm up in front of the body. The right "V" hand is placed in a standing position on the left palm.

STAND (FOR A LONG TIME) - "I stood near the tree for a long time."
Make the sign for STAND and move it in a continuous circular motion.

Practice

Practice Sentences for You to Try

Remember to use the modified movement for the verbs.

ENGLISH	GLOSS FOR ASL
You played a lot today.	TODAY YOU PLAY PLAY PLAY
I don't like to sit for a long time.	ME SIT SIT SIT DON'T-LIKE
Daddy has been sick a lot.	DADDY SICK SICK SICK
You laughed and laughed at that funny movie.	MOVIE FUNNY YOU LAUGH LAUGH
Mommy has a really bad headache.	MOMMY HURT HURT HURT (use the HURT sign repeated near the head)
I don't want to wait for a long time.	ME WAIT WAIT DON'T-WANT
You've been watching TV for a long long time.	TV YOU WATCH (circle movement)
It rained and rained today.	TODAY RAIN RAIN RAIN
Your brother has a lot of studying to do.	YOUR BROTHER STUDY STUDY MUST
Your brother eats a lot.	YOUR BROTHER EAT EAT EAT

Activities

Watch your child's actions and, whenever appropriate, use the temporal aspect to comment on his/her activity.

EXAMPLES:
If your child is staring at something, comment by signing:
YOU LOOK/STARE (point the "V" handshape , palm down, toward whatever is being looked at)

If you see a family member reading a book, you can tell your child:
HE (point) BOOK READ READ

If you are in a situation where you have to wait for a long time, explain to your child:
WE WAIT WAIT WAIT MUST

If it has been raining all day you can comment on that by signing:
RAIN RAIN RAIN ALL-DAY
It has rained and rained all day.

At mealtime if someone is still eating after everyone else has finished, you can comment on that by signing:

ENGLISH	GLOSS FOR ASL
I have eaten.	ME EAT FINISH
You have eaten.	YOU EAT FINISH
He is eating.	HE (point) EAT EAT EAT

Unit 7

Word Order

Several principles guide word order, or syntax, in ASL. The next few chapters will cover the:

TOPIC—COMMENT PRINCIPLE
ASL is a topic-comment language. This means that most of the time the topic is signed first, then the comment about the topic is signed.

NOUN—ADJECTIVE RELATIONSHIP
Most of the time in ASL the noun is signed first followed by the adjective.

THREE-SIGNS-OR-LESS PRINCIPLE
If a sentence has three signs or less, the signs can usually be arranged in any order.

TIME INDICATORS
Usually, time indicators are signed first in ASL. Time indicators in ASL are signs that let you know when something took place or will take place.

TIME SEQUENCE PRINCIPLE
ASL usually requires that events are signed in the order in which they occur. Whatever happened first is signed first.

Lesson 18
Topic-Comment Principle

ASL is primarily a topic-comment language. This means that in most cases, the topic you wish to discuss is signed first and the comment about the topic follows. This is different from English because in English the comments often come before the topic.

Most of the time, in ASL, signs such as WANT, DON'T-WANT, MUST (HAVE TO, NEED), WILL, LIKE, DON'T-LIKE, CAN, CAN'T, and WON'T (REFUSE) will come after the topic because they are used as comments about the topic.

EXAMPLES:

ENGLISH	GLOSS FOR ASL
I want a new car.	CAR NEW WANT ME (In ASL the topic, car, would come first, followed by the comments.)
The boy broke the window.	WINDOW BOY BROKE
Your room needs cleaning.	ROOM YOUR CLEAN NEED
You have a new dress.	DRESS NEW YOU HAVE
Those flowers are pretty.	FLOWERS (point) PRETTY
You can't play.	YOU PLAY CAN'T
I need a drink.	DRINK NEED
I can drive.	ME DRIVE CAN
Brother won't share.	BROTHER SHARE REFUSE

Practice
Practice Sentences for You to Try

ENGLISH	GLOSS FOR ASL
I don't like chocolate.	CHOCOLATE DON'T-LIKE ME
I have to go to the bathroom.	ME BATHROOM NEED
You can't go outside.	OUTSIDE GO CAN'T
She won't give me the book.	BOOK GIVE-ME SHE (point) REFUSE
I will find your shoes.	SHOES YOUR FIND WILL
You can play in your room.	YOUR ROOM (point) PLAY CAN
I can't read now.	NOW ME READ CAN'T
Dad will be home later.	LATER DAD ARRIVE HOME WILL
You can't go to school today.	TODAY SCHOOL GO CAN'T
I need to go.	ME GO MUST
You can watch TV now.	NOW TV YOU WATCH CAN

Activities

You will find that the topic-comment principle is helpful in getting and keeping your child's attention. Instead of signing each word in English as in, "Do you want a cookie?" ASL allows the topic, COOKIE to be signed first which gets your child's attention, then you ask the question or make a comment.

1. Watch carefully what your child is doing and comment on it. Remember, the topic is signed first, then the comment.

ENGLISH	GLOSS FOR ASL
You are feeding the doll.	DOLL YOU FEED
You are petting the dog.	DOG YOU PET
You are reading the book.	BOOK YOU READ
You are drawing a pretty picture.	PICTURE YOU DRAW PRETTY

2. Comment on what you are doing or what you and your child are doing together.

ENGLISH	GLOSS FOR ASL
I have to wash many dishes.	DISHES MANY WASH HAVE TO
I have to vacuum this dirty floor.	FLOOR DIRTY VACUUM NEED
You pick up the books.	BOOKS YOU PICK-UP
Let's make a peanut butter sandwich.	SANDWICH PEANUT BUTTER MAKE
You eat the peanut butter sandwich.	YOU SANDWICH PEANUT BUTTER EAT

3. Go for walks with your child and talk about what is going on around you.

ENGLISH	GLOSS FOR ASL
The boy is climbing the tree.	TREE BOY CLIMB
There are lots of cars here.	CARS MANY HERE
The little dog is running.	DOG SMALL RUN
There are many men working.	MEN MANY WORK

4. Use the topic-comment principle to talk about what is on TV.

ENGLISH	GLOSS FOR ASL
The woman is sad and crying.	WOMAN SAD CRY
The men are playing football.	MEN FOOTBALL PLAY
The boy hit the ball.	BOY BALL HIT
The elephant is big.	ELEPHANT BIG

5. Emphasize the topic-comment principle as you look at picture books or photo albums with your child.

ENGLISH	GLOSS FOR ASL
Daddy has on funny clothes.	DADDY CLOTHES FUNNY
Sister blew out the candles.	SISTER CANDLES BLOW
The girl has many cats.	GIRL CATS MANY HAVE
Mom's dress is pretty.	MOM DRESS PRETTY

Lesson 19
Noun-Adjective Relationship

Most of the time in ASL the noun is signed first followed by the adjective.

EXAMPLES:

ENGLISH	GLOSS FOR ASL
I have a blue car.	CAR BLUE HAVE
I want the red ball.	BALL RED WANT
I want three eggs.	EGGS 3 WANT
I have five books.	BOOKS 5 HAVE
My shirt is dirty.	SHIRT MINE DIRTY
I like silly stories.	STORIES SILLY LIKE
The broken window is dangerous.	WINDOW BROKEN DANGEROUS
The black dog is hungry.	DOG BLACK HUNGRY
My white horse is big.	MY HORSE WHITE BIG
My sister has a new red bike.	SISTER MINE BIKE NEW RED HAVE

Practice

Practice Sentences for You to Try

ENGLISH	GLOSS FOR ASL
I see pretty clouds.	CLOUDS PRETTY SEE
I have a brown dog.	DOG BROWN HAVE
I want two eggs.	EGGS 2 WANT
Do you want the blue ball?	BALL BLUE WANT (Q-y/n)
Do you like tiny cars?	CARS TINY LIKE (Q-y/n)
Do you want more juice?	JUICE MORE WANT (Q-y/n)
Sister has many books.	SISTER BOOKS MANY HAVE
Daddy likes green vegetables.	DADDY VEGETABLES GREEN LIKE
I want some new white shoes.	SHOES NEW WHITE WANT
Do you have a blue pen?	PEN BLUE HAVE (Q-y/n)
I saw a big brown horse.	I SEE HORSE BROWN BIG
Give me the blue cup.	CUP BLUE YOU-GIVE-ME
Show me your new shoes.	SHOES NEW YOU-SHOW-ME

Activities

1. There are so many things that can be described when you go places with your child. You can go for a walk, to the store, to the park, or to the zoo and find many opportunities to practice noun-adjective combinations in ASL.

ENGLISH	GLOSS FOR ASL
The clouds are pretty.	CLOUDS PRETTY
There is a little black bird.	BIRD LITTLE BLACK (point)
The window is broken.	WINDOW BROKEN
There is a pretty yellow flower.	FLOWER YELLOW PRETTY (point)
The wall is dirty and ugly.	WALL DIRTY UGLY
The little dog is cute.	DOG LITTLE CUTE
The silly monkey is jumping.	MONKEY SILLY JUMP
The grass is wet.	GRASS WET

2. Mealtime is a great time to practice noun-adjective combinations. You can practice using noun-adjective combinations and the topic-comment principle together.

	TOPIC NOUN-ADJECTIVE	COMMENT
I want two pieces of toast.	TOAST TWO	ME WANT PLEASE
You have one potato.	POTATO ONE	YOU HAVE
I want three cookies.	COOKIES THREE	ME WANT
Sorry, there are no apples.	APPLE NONE	SORRY
We are out of milk. We need more.	MILK NONE	NEED MORE

3. When your child is playing, especially when colors or numbers are involved, emphasize the use of noun-adjective combinations and the topic-comment principle.

	TOPIC NOUN-ADJECTIVE	COMMENT
You have three trucks.	TRUCKS THREE	YOU HAVE
You like the red crayon.	CRAYON RED	YOU LIKE
You drew a pretty picture.	PICTURE PRETTY	YOU DRAW
You have a big pillow.	PILLOW BIG	YOU HAVE
You need a warm jacket.	JACKET WARM	YOU NEED

4. Noun-adjective combinations can be used frequently when looking through books or picture albums with your child.

ENGLISH	GLOSS FOR ASL
There is a big black horse.	HORSE BLACK BIG (point)
That rabbit is silly.	RABBIT SILLY (point)
Brother has lots of presents.	BROTHER PRESENTS MANY HAVE
There are many blue and red bicycles.	BICYCLES RED BLUE MANY
Daddy fell and got hurt.	DADDY FALL HURT

5. Play guessing games with your child. Give adjective hints, for example:

YOU:	SMALL RED ROUND (for geometric shapes, trace the shape in the air using the index finger)
CHILD:	MY BALL
YOU:	YES! BALL SMALL RED ROUND
YOU:	PRETTY YELLOW SMELL GOOD
CHILD:	MOMMY FLOWER
YOU:	YES! MOMMY FLOWER PRETTY YELLOW SMELL GOOD

6. When you go grocery shopping with your child, you can use your grocery list to practice noun-adjective combinations.

ENGLISH	GLOSS FOR ASL
We need four bananas.	BANANAS FOUR NEED
We need six apples.	APPLES SIX NEED
We need two gallons of milk.	MILK TWO NEED
We don't need any eggs.	EGGS DON'T NEED

Lesson 20
Three-Signs-or-Less Principle

You have learned a few basic principles that govern word order in ASL. As with any language, there are exceptions to the rule. The three-signs-or-less principle is helpful to know so that you don't feel restricted with how you arrange your signs in short sentences.

When a sentence has three signs or less, most of the time the signs can be arranged in any order.

The important thing to remember is that ASL is an efficient language, meaning the signs flow together easily so that there is not a lot of unnecessary movement. You can say it is a visual and kinesthetic language. The movements are pleasing to the eye and comfortable to produce.

Practice
Practice Sentences for You to Try

ENGLISH	GLOSS FOR ASL
▣ I have a box.	BOX ME HAVE
	ME HAVE BOX
	BOX HAVE ME
▣ I like apples.	APPLES ME LIKE
	ME LIKE APPLES
	APPLES LIKE ME
▣ I want to go.	GO WANT ME
	ME WANT GO
	ME GO WANT
▣ I don't like coffee.	COFFEE ME DON'T-LIKE
	ME DON'T-LIKE COFFEE
	ME COFFEE DON'T-LIKE

Practice Making Your Own Sentences

Use the combination of words below to make basic sentences in ASL. Choose one word from each column to make your sentences.

FRIEND	WANT	GAME
BROTHER	DON'T WANT	COOKIES
SISTER	LIKE	PLAY
MOM	DON'T LIKE	READ
DAD	MUST, HAVE-TO	FLOWERS
GRANDMA	NEED	ORANGE JUICE
I, ME	SHOULD	HELP
YOU	HAVE	DRINK
GRANDPA		GO
AUNT		DRAW
UNCLE		RUN

Activities

Review some of the activities that were included in previous chapters. Be aware of times when your sentence has three signs or less. You can practice changing the sign order and notice which structure feels most comfortable.

Try these sentences and decide which choice feels the smoothest and flows together the best:

ENGLISH	GLOSS FOR ASL
The girl went home.	GIRL GO HOME
	GIRL HOME GO
The boy is eating a banana.	BOY EAT BANANA
	BANANA BOY EAT
	BOY BANANA EAT
The girl is reading a book.	GIRL BOOK READ
	BOOK GIRL READ
	GIRL READ BOOK
Mom is a good cook.	MOM COOK GOOD
	MOM GOOD COOK
Brother has a book.	BOOK BROTHER HAVE
	BROTHER BOOK HAVE
	BROTHER HAVE BOOK

Lesson 21
Time Indicators

Time indicators in ASL are signs that let you know when something took place, is taking place, or will take place. These signs typically come at the beginning of the sentence.

A portion of the following time indicators are shown on the instructional videotape.

tomorrow	yesterday	next week	last week
today	morning	afternoon	night
weekly	last year	next year	this week
this month	monthly	yearly	this year
fall	spring	summer	winter
now	later	soon	recently
every month	every Monday	every Tuesday	every Wednesday
every Thursday	every Friday	every Saturday	every Sunday
daily			

EXAMPLES:

ENGLISH	GLOSS FOR ASL
We will see Grandma tomorrow.	TOMORROW GRANDMA SEE WILL
We go to church every Sunday.	WEEKLY SUNDAY CHURCH GO
You go to school every day.	DAILY YOU SCHOOL GO

Practice

Practice Sentences for You to Master

Remember to use the other rules you have learned about ASL word order (topic-comment, noun-adjective, and three-signs-or-less principle) when signing these sentences.

ENGLISH	GLOSS FOR ASL
School starts next week.	NEXT WEEK SCHOOL BEGIN
Daddy will not go to work tomorrow.	TOMORROW DADDY NOT GO WORK (shake head "no")
Your uncle is coming this afternoon.	NOW-AFTERNOON YOUR UNCLE COME WILL
Last year you were four years old.	LAST YEAR YOU AGE-4
We have hot dogs every Friday.	WEEKLY FRIDAY WE EAT HOT DOGS
We will go to the store later.	LATER STORE GO WILL
You need to eat your sandwich now.	NOW SANDWICH YOU EAT MUST
We went to the park yesterday.	YESTERDAY PARK GO
Next week is your birthday.	NEXT WEEK YOUR BIRTHDAY

Activities

1. Getting up and going to bed routines are good times to talk about "time." For example, what will happen, what happened that day, etc.

GETTING UP
ENGLISH

This afternoon you have gymnastics.

This evening Grandma is coming over.
Your class will go to the zoo today.
Would you like to help Daddy wash the car this morning?

GOING TO BED
ENGLISH

This morning you helped Mommy cook breakfast.

After lunch you played on the swing.

Tomorrow you have school.
Tomorrow night we will go see Sister's play.

You helped clean up after supper tonight.

GLOSS FOR ASL

NOW AFTERNOON GYMNASTICS CLASS YOU HAVE

NOW EVENING GRANDMA COME

TODAY CLASS YOUR ZOO GO WILL

NOW MORNING CAR DADDY WASH YOU HELP DADDY WANT (Q-y/n)

GLOSS FOR ASL

NOW MORNING YOU HELP MOMMY BREAKFAST COOK

NOW DAY NOON EAT FINISH (pause) YOU PLAY SWING

TOMORROW SCHOOL YOU GO MUST

TOMORROW NIGHT SISTER DRAMA GO SEE

TONIGHT EAT FINISH YOU HELP CLEAN-UP

2. During the day, in daily conversation, focus on comments about time.

ENGLISH

What do you want to do this afternoon?

This morning you left the milk out on the counter.

GLOSS FOR ASL

NOW AFTERNOON YOU WANT DO (Q/wh)

NOW MORNING MILK LEAVE TABLE YOU

3. Get a calendar or a clock so that you and your child can frequently discuss the concept of time. Mark special events on your child's calendar.

ENGLISH

Your birthday is next month.

Grandma will visit in two weeks.
Daddy will be home at 4:00.
We have to leave at 2:30.
You have to wake up early tomorrow morning.

GLOSS FOR ASL

NEXT MONTH HAPPEN (Q-y/n) YOUR BIRTHDAY

TWO-WEEKS-FUTURE GRANDMA COME WILL

TIME 4 DADDY ARRIVE HOME

TIME 2:30 WE LEAVE MUST

TOMORROW MORNING EARLY YOU WAKE-UP MUST

101

4. You might like to have a "household task" calendar. The calendar would show different jobs that members of the family do on different days or at different times. You can use the calendar to practice using time indicators such as days of the week, clock time, morning, afternoon, and evening.

Task	Sun	Mon	Tue	Wed	Thu	Fri	Sat
wash dishes	Mom	Mom	Caren	Caren	Billy	Billy	Mom
dry dishes	Billy	Caren	Mom	Mom	Caren	Caren	Billy
dust	Billy	Mom	Caren	Caren	Mom	Mom	Billy
set table	Dad	Dad	Billy	Caren	Mom	Mom	Dad
feed Patches	Dad	Dad	Dad	Billy	Billy	Dad	Billy

Lesson 22
Time Sequence Principle

With English we don't always report things in the order that they happened or will happen. For example, in English, we may say something like this:

1. You need to help me clean up as soon as you finish eating.
2. Daddy will wash the car after the football game.

With ASL, however, events are usually described in the order in which they occur or will occur. Whatever happened first is signed first.

1. YOU EAT FINISH* HELP-ME CLEAN NEED
2. FOOTBALL GAME FINISH* DADDY CAR WASH WILL

*Usually there is a pause after the FINISH sign to show a break between events or activities. Sometimes a body shift may even be used to alter the signing space slightly; this also shows a change in events or activities.

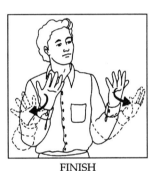

FINISH

Practice

Practice Sentences for You to Try

ENGLISH	GLOSS FOR ASL
We will go get ice cream after the movie.	MOVIE FINISH ICE CREAM GET WILL
You can go outside and play when Daddy gets home.	HAPPEN DADDY ARRIVE HOME YOU PLAY OUTSIDE CAN
We will eat after the baseball game.	BASEBALL GAME FINISH EAT WILL
Your sister cried when Mom left.	HAPPEN MOM LEAVE (pause) YOUR SISTER (point) CRY CRY
Daddy is sick after eating so much candy.	DADDY CANDY EAT EAT EAT FINISH NOW SICK
We will ride our bikes when it stops raining.	RAIN FINISH (pause) WE BIKE-RIDE WILL
Jimmy walked home because he didn't see Mom's car after school.	JIMMY SCHOOL FINISH (pause) MOM CAR SEE NOT (pause) CL: 1 WALK HOME
You can have some pie after you finish your supper.	YOU EAT FINISH (pause) P-I-E YOU HAVE CAN

Activities

1. During the morning routine (getting up, getting dressed, and eating breakfast) is a good time to talk about what will happen that day. Remember to use the ASL time sequence principle and sign things in the order that they happened or will happen.

ENGLISH	GLOSS FOR ASL
We will go to Grandma's after lunch.	NOON EAT FINISH GRANDMA HOUSE WE GO WILL
This morning we will go shopping after breakfast.	NOW MORNING EAT FINISH SHOPPING GO WE WILL
You can play outside after we go shopping.	SHOPPING FINISH YOU PLAY OUTSIDE CAN

2. Getting ready for bed is a good time to review with your child what happened during the day and practice using the time sequence principle.

ENGLISH	GLOSS FOR ASL
We saw the rabbit after the rain this morning.	NOW MORNING RAIN FINISH RABBIT WE SAW
We got ice cream after Cindy came home from school.	SCHOOL FINISH CINDY COME 3-OF-US ICE CREAM GET

3. Before going on an errand, discuss the sequence of events with your child using the time sequence principle.

ENGLISH	GLOSS FOR ASL
We will go the post office after we go to the grocery store; then we will go see Grandma.	NOW WE FOOD STORE GO FINISH (pause) POST OFFICE GO FINISH (pause) GRANDMA HOUSE GO

4. Arrange to go on a special walk or trip with your child such as going for a hamburger or to the park. Plan some events that your child will remember. When you return, discuss with your child what happened.

After returning from any event such as a visit to a friend's house, the dentist, or school, you can take a few minutes to discuss what happened using the time sequence principle.

ENGLISH	GLOSS FOR ASL
We played on the swing after we fed the ducks.	WE DUCKS FEED FINISH PLAY SWING
We played on the slide after we had our hamburgers.	WE HAMBURGERS EAT FINISH PLAY SLIDE
We got some ice cream after playing.	WE PLAY PLAY FINISH GET ICE CREAM

5. Review the activities listed for the chapters on Number Incorporation (page 116-117) and Time Indicators (page 101-102), and practice working the time sequence principle into those activities.

Unit 8

Sign Modification

All languages allow for colorful changes to basic statements in order to add new information or varying degrees of intensity.

In English we may describe something using words such as pretty, beautiful, or gorgeous. We may also add words such as very, somewhat, or not to change the meaning. We may also change the inflection in our voices to change the meaning of a word.

ASL is no exception. It too allows for changes in meaning of basic statements and varying degrees of intensity when expressing ideas.

ASL is a very efficient language. The signs are arranged in a way that economizes energy and movement. Many times the meanings of signs can be changed by altering the movement or facial expression slightly without the use of any additional words or signs.

Some examples of this include:
   Modifying signs with movement;
   Modifying signs with facial expression;
   Using number incorporation on a sign.

Lesson 23
Showing Different Meanings by Altering Facial Expression and Movement of the Sign

ASL is a colorful, descriptive language. People often mistakenly think that ASL has only one sign for one concept, whereas English has many words to describe concepts. This is not true. An example of this are the degrees of beauty which English is able to describe: pretty, lovely, gorgeous, stunning, etc. In comparison, ASL also has the capability of expressing many degrees of intensity. Because ASL is a visual language, however, these changes in degree of intensity happen visually on the face and body.

The intensity and resultant meaning of a sign can be altered completely by either changing facial expressions or the movement of the sign or both.

EXAMPLES:
NOW   The sign is made casually in front of the body.
RIGHT NOW   The sign is made closer to the body with more tenseness in the arms.
IMMEDIATE   The sign is made very close to the body and the arms are extremely tense.
            (Facial expression is also used to show more urgency.)

Altering the Meaning of Signs by Modifying Movement

Changing the movement of a sign, by slowing it down, speeding it up, making it larger, or making it smaller, can show degrees of intensity. In fact, the movement can completely change the meaning of a sign.

Modifying Signs Using Facial Expressions

Facial expressions are a crucial part of ASL. In your videotape, you will notice that some sort of facial expression is used with practically everything that is signed. The use of appropriate facial expressions cannot be emphasized enough!

Facial expressions can be used to alter a sign slightly or to change its meaning drastically.

Some facial expressions, when combined with certain signs, can totally change the meaning of the sign. Depend on examples in your videotape to model expressions for you.

109

The following examples shown on the practice sentences videotape will demonstrate how movement of a sign and facial expression can be altered to change meaning.

EXAMPLES:

▮ WALKING SLOWLY (CL:1 is used, refer to Lesson 14)
▮ WALKING AIMLESSLY (CL:1 is used, refer to Lesson 14)

▮ WORKING DILIGENTLY
▮ WORKING LACKADAISICALLY

▮ EATING SLOWLY
▮ EATING QUICKLY

▮ SITTING NERVOUSLY
▮ SITTING BORED FOR A LONG TIME

▮ FINE WITH ME
▮ NOT FINE WITH ME

▮ STUDY FOR A LONG TIME

▮ SLIGHT HEADACHE
▮ NAGGING HEADACHE
▮ A SHARP PAIN

Practice

Practice using facial expression and movement to show the difference between these synonyms.

pretty / beautiful
tired / exhausted
angry / furious
bored / bored to tears
ugly / very ugly
work happily / work grudgingly
funny / hilarious
many people / hoards of people

Practice Sentences

(Not shown on video...sorry!)

The gloss seems very dry written out, so remember to use appropriate facial expression!

ENGLISH	GLOSS FOR ASL
Daddy is working hard.	DADDY WORK
Sister doesn't like soup.	SOUP SISTER DON'T LIKE
I can't go and I am mad.	ME GO CAN'T ANGRY ME
I love ice cream.	ICE CREAM I LOVE
My dog is sick.	DOG MINE SICK
You must sit down now.	SIT NOW MUST

Activities

1. See how many different ways family members can sign a descriptor such as UGLY, PRETTY, or OLD, to show different degrees and meanings. Concentrate on altering facial expression and movement of the sign.

tired	very tired	exhausted
funny	really funny	hilarious
cry	cry a lot	bawl eyes out
happy	very happy	thrilled
mad	very angry	furious

2. Play a guessing game. Have a family member think of someone or something. Then give the clues which will lead to the identity of the person, place, or thing. Be creative!

CLUE:	ANSWER:
MAN REALLY REALLY FUNNY	UNCLE BEN
DOG BARK VERY VERY LOUD	PATCHES
MOVIE REALLY REALLY SCARY	DRACULA
BOY STUDY HARD (MM expression)	DAVID
GIRL DRIVE CARELESSLY (TH)	BETTY

3. Remember to use different degrees of facial expression and sign intensity as you communicate with your child in various daily routines.

While washing dishes, you could sign:
CUP DIRTY
PLATE VERY DIRTY
WATER REALLY HOT

While cleaning up the room, you could sign:
ROOM MESSY
CLOSET VERY MESSY
TOYS MANY EVERY WHERE (point)

While working in the garden, you could sign:
FLOWER PRETTY
FLOWER BEAUTIFUL
SQUASH BIG
PUMPKIN HUGE

While cooking meals, you could sign:
SUGAR GOOD
CHOCOLATE BITTER
ICING REALLY GOOD

Lesson 24
Number Incorporation

ASL is a smooth, efficient language; whenever possible the rules allow for the elimination of unnecessary movement. Such is the case with what is called number incorporation onto a sign. Rather than signing two separate signs for a number and a noun, some signs allow for the number to be incorporated right onto the sign itself. Examples of this principle are demonstrated on your videotape.

AGE
For ages 1-9, the number moves from the chin down in front of the body.

For ages above 9, the sign for OLD is signed followed by the number.

WEEKS
For numbers 1-9, the number can be incorporated with the sign for WEEK.

For numbers 10 and above, both the NUMBER sign and the WEEK sign are used.

Number incorporation can also be used to indicate how many weeks ago an event occurred or how many weeks into the future an event will occur: TWO WEEKS FROM NOW, or TWO WEEKS AGO. Consult your videotape for examples.

YEARS
For 1-5 years from now, the number can become part of the YEAR sign as it moves into the future.

For 1-5 years ago, the number can become part of the sign YEAR as it moves into the past.

Numbers greater than 5 require you to sign the number, then the YEAR sign, then indicate future or past.

Take a quick look at your videotape to clear up any misunderstanding.

MONTHS
For numbers 1-9, the number can become part of the MONTH sign by letting the number handshape slide down the left index finger as in the MONTH sign.

For numbers greater than 9, the number must be made separately from the MONTH sign. Signs such as future or past are made separately.

113

HOURS
To show the length of an occurrence in hours, you can sign the HOUR sign and then add a number.

For the numbers 1-5, however, you can incorporate the number with the HOUR sign: 2 hours, 3 hours, 4 hours, etc.

"WE"
Although there is a sign for WE that moves from shoulder to shoulder with the index finger, when you want to indicate a specific number of people, this can be done with number incorporation onto a sign.

2-OF-US
This sign is made with a "K" position, palm up, moving back and forth from yourself to the other person.

3-OF-US
This sign is made with the "3" position, palm up, using a circular movement.

4-OF-US
This sign is made with the "4" position, palm up, using a circular movement.

5-OF-US
This sign is made with the "5" position, palm up, using a circular movement.

Practice
Practice Sentences for You to Try

ENGLISH	GLOSS FOR ASL
You will be five years old next year.	NEXT-YEAR YOU AGE-5 WILL
Your birthday is two months away.	2-MONTHS FUTURE YOUR BIRTHDAY
The three of us will play a game.	3-OF-US GAME PLAY WILL
You two stop arguing.	2-OF-YOU ARGUE FINISH
School will be out in two weeks.	2-WEEKS-FUTURE SCHOOL FINISH
Last year we went to Disneyland.	1-YEAR AGO FAMILY GO D-I-S-N-E-Y-L-A-N-D
Mom has to leave in a couple of hours.	2-HOURS FUTURE MOM LEAVE MUST
Bobby is six years old.	BOBBY AGE-SIX
Jimmy is in school seven hours everyday.	DAILY JIMMY SCHOOL GO STAY HOURS 7
The football game was on for two hours.	TV FOOTBALL GAME 2-HOURS CONTINUE WILL
That movie will last for three hours.	MOVIE (point) 3-HOURS CONTINUE WILL
The three of us can share.	3-OF-US SHARE CAN

Activities

1. Concentrate on using number incorporation in your daily conversations with your child.

ENGLISH	GLOSS FOR ASL
We need to go in three hours.	3-HOURS-FUTURE WE LEAVE MUST
That TV show was two hours long.	TV MOVIE 2-HOURS CONTINUE
You lost your toy two weeks ago.	2-WEEKS-AGO TOY YOUR LOST

2. Use number incorporation as you discuss special events with your child. For example, discuss special events that are on the calendar.

ENGLISH	GLOSS FOR ASL
It will be Christmas in three weeks.	3-WEEKS-FUTURE CHRISTMAS
Grandpa's birthday was two weeks ago.	2-WEEKS-AGO GRANDPA BIRTHDAY
Last year, we hunted Easter eggs at Grandma's.	1-YEAR-AGO EASTER GRANDMA HOUSE WE EGGS SEARCH

3. Make a seasons book with your child. You can use a notebook or photo album and label a section of it for each season. Include a twelve-month calendar, pictures of each season, and pictures of special activities you did during that season. You can use this book to practice using number incorporation.

You can use the calendar to count how many more weeks or months before the season change or a special event takes place.

ENGLISH	GLOSS FOR ASL
It will be winter in three months.	3-MONTHS FUTURE HAPPEN WINTER
We can build a snowman four months from now.	4-MONTHS FUTURE SNOWMAN CAN MAKE
We went swimming two months ago.	2-MONTHS PAST WE SWIM
The leaves will change colors in one more month.	1-MONTH FUTURE TREE LEAVES CHANGE COLOR
Last week we had Caren's birthday party.	1-WEEK-AGO CAREN BIRTHDAY PARTY

4. When discussing what will happen at different times during the day, remember to use number incorporation.

ENGLISH	GLOSS FOR ASL
We will eat in two hours.	2 HOURS FUTURE EAT WILL
Daddy will be home in three hours.	3 HOURS DADDY HOME WILL
Your dance class is in four hours.	4 HOURS FUTURE DANCE CLASS YOU

5. Talk about the ages of persons when looking in books or magazines, or play a guessing game trying to guess the age of the person in the picture.

ENGLISH	GLOSS FOR ASL
He looks about 60 years old.	HE (point) LOOK ABOUT OLD 60
I think that little girl is three years old.	GIRL LITTLE (show height with palm down) AGE-3
How old do you think he is?	HE (point) OLD (Q-wh)
Response: six years old.	Response: OLD-6

6. When looking through a family photo album or your child's experience book, focus on the time that events happened and comment about it using number incorporation.

ENGLISH	GLOSS FOR ASL
That was Daddy's birthday. It was two months ago.	THAT (point) 2-MONTHS PAST DADDY BIRTHDAY
Oh, that is when we went to Florida two years ago.	THERE (point) 2-YEARS-AGO WE GO FLORIDA
Yes, we made ice cream six months ago.	6-MONTHS PAST WE ICE CREAM MAKE

7. Remember to use the variations of "we" such as 2-of-us or 3-of-us when the opportunity comes up during the day.

ENGLISH	GLOSS FOR ASL
You and I can set the table.	2-OF-US SET TABLE (move "K" handshape, palm up, back and forth between you and child)
Daddy and Jimmy can get the chairs.	2-OF-THEM CHAIRS GET (move "K" handshape, palm up, back and forth between Dad and Jimmy)

Unit 9

Other Topics

ASL is a language with many and diverse topics which could easily encompass several volumes. This book thus far has provided you with tools to facilitate your grasping a basic understanding of the language. Included in this unit, "Other Topics," are pertinent areas of information that will further enhance your learning of American Sign Language.

Lesson 25
Plurality

As you know, to show plurality in English we add -s or -es to words or change the spelling: dog - dogs, man - men. In ASL plurality is indicated differently.

PLURALITY INDICATED BY CONTEXT ALONE
In many instances the context alone dictates plurality of a sign; nothing more is needed to clarify that plurality is intended.

For example, if you sign the gloss for ASL: DOG - I - LIKE, the English translation would be:
I like dogs.
The plural of dog is implied by the context of the sentence.

TO SPECIFICALLY INDICATE THE SINGULAR FORM OF NOUNS
If you wanted to be more specific and indicate a certain dog, the singular form, you would need to index or point to the space in front of you after signing dog.

For example, if you sign the gloss for ASL: DOG (point) - I - LIKE; the English translation would be:
I like that dog.

TO SPECIFICALLY INDICATE THE PLURAL FORM OF NOUNS
Other than using context to imply plurality, there are three ways to specifically indicate plurality in ASL.

1. INDEXING
This word simply means that you point your index finger several times in the space in front of you after you sign the noun.

DOG	Sign DOG and point one time to the space in front of you.
3 DOGS	Sign DOG and point 3 times to the space in from of you, moving left to right.
CAT	Sign CAT and point one time to the space in front of you.
CATS	Sign CAT and point a few times to the space in front of you, moving left to right.
MAN	Sign MAN and point one time to the space in front of you.
MEN	Sign MAN and point a few times to the space in front of you, moving left to right.

2. USING A NUMBER OR WORD TO INDICATE MORE THAN ONE
   This means that in your sentence you will use a number or a specific word such as MANY, SEVERAL, FEW, or SOME to show that the noun is plural.

   These examples use specific words and numbers to show plurality:

ENGLISH	GLOSS FOR ASL
three dogs	DOG 3
many cats	CAT MANY
a few men	MAN FEW
more cookies	COOKIE MORE
some boys	BOY SOME
two boys	BOY 2

3. Some signs, though not many, will allow another way to indicate plurality: repeating the sign.

   EXAMPLE:

ENGLISH	GLOSS FOR ASL
I have 3 books.	BOOK BOOK BOOK HAVE ME
	(repeat the sign BOOK from left to right in front of you)

   Classifiers also allow for repeating the sign to show plurality and are more commonly repeated for plurality than are specific signs.

ENGLISH	GLOSS FOR ASL
The cars were parked side by side in a row.	C-A-R (spell car) CL:VEHICLE (3) (repeat) (repeat the classifier several times moving left to right in front of your body to show how they were parked)
My coat has three buttons.	COAT MINE CL:F (repeat the classifier 3 times moving down the front of your body)

Practice

Practice Sentences for You to Try

With these sentences, the plural form is implied by the context, so just use the sign as is.

ENGLISH	GLOSS FOR ASL
I like to read books.	BOOK READ I-LIKE
Mom made cookies.	COOKIE MOM MAKE
	-*or*- MOM MAKE COOKIE
My sister plays with dolls.	MY SISTER PLAY WITH DOLL
How many brothers do you have?	BROTHER MANY HAVE (Q-wh)
Sometimes cats are mean.	SOMETIMES CAT MEAN

For these sentences, try using indexing to indicate plurality. Remember to point to thes-space in front of you after the noun.

ENGLISH	GLOSS FOR ASL
Are those books yours?	BOOK (point a few times) YOUR (Q-y/n)
Those three boys are in my class.	BOY (point 3 times) IN MY CLASS
The men are here to help us.	MAN (point a few times) HERE HELP-US WILL
Bring those dolls to me.	DOLL (point to them) YOU GIVE-ME

For the next practice sentences, add the specific word or number after the noun to show plurality.

ENGLISH	GLOSS FOR ASL
I have seen a lot of movies.	MOVIE MANY SEE FINISH ME
There are six boys in our class.	OUR CLASS BOY 6 HAVE
A few students are not here.	STUDENT FEW NOT HERE
I want to read two books.	BOOK 2 READ WANT

Repeat the sign or classifier to show plurality in the following sentences:

ENGLISH	GLOSS FOR ASL
I need three cups.	(CL:C) CUP CUP CUP (repeat three times) NEED ME
I see three cars.	CAR (CL:3 repeat three times) SEE
I need three balls to juggle.	BALL BALL BALL NEED (mime juggling)
I am looking for cups.	CUP CUP CUP (CL: C) I SEARCH
My family has two cars.	C-A-R (CL: 3 repeated twice) FAMILY MINE HAVE
The 2 boys walked along.	BOY (move CL:2 in front of you)
Which book do you want?	BOOK BOOK WHICH WANT (Q-wh)

More Practice Sentences for You to Try

Now try practicing the sentences again, choosing your own way to show plurality.
Using context alone
Indexing
Repeating sign
Using a word or number

Sign each sentence twice, choosing a different way to show plurality each time.
Remember that some of the ways to show plurality will not always work with some of the
sentences.

ENGLISH	GLOSS FOR ASL
I like to read books.	BOOKS READ LIKE
My sister plays with dolls.	DOLLS MY SISTER PLAY
How many brothers do you have?	BROTHER MANY HAVE YOU (Q-wh)
Sometimes cats are mean.	SOMETIMES CAT MEAN
Mom made cookies.	MOM COOKIE MAKE FINISH
Are those books yours?	BOOK (index) YOUR(Q-y/n)
Those three boys are in my class.	BOYS 3 (index) IN MY CLASS
The men are here to help us.	MAN HERE HELP US
Bring those apples to me.	APPLE BRING-TO-ME
A few students are not here.	STUDENT FEW NOT HERE
I have seen a lot of movies.	MOVIE MANY SEE
There are six boys in our class.	BOY 6 IN OUR CLASS
I want to read two books.	BOOK 2 READ WANT
I need three balls.	3 BALL NEED
I am looking for cups.	CUP LOOKING-FOR
My family has two cars.	FAMILY MY CAR 2 HAVE
The two boys walked along.	BOY 2 WALK
Which book do you want?	BOOK WANT WHICH (Q-wh)

Activities

1. A visit to the grocery store is a good opportunity to practice singular and plural nouns.

> EXAMPLES:
> KOOL-AID PKGS MANY NEED
> KETCHUP ONE NEED (point to it)
> BANANA FEW NEED
> WATERMELON ONE NEED
> APPLES 4 NEED

2. When your child is playing with his toys, use that opportunity to point out plural and singular nouns using one of the ways of indicating plurals that you have practiced.

> EXAMPLES:
> RED BALL 2 YOU HAVE
> YELLOW BALL MANY
> BLUE BALL ONE

3. Look at pictures of people, your family, school class pictures, or pictures in magazines, and comment on the people using plurality.

> EXAMPLES:
> MAN MANY
> CHILDREN MANY
> GIRL (point)
> LADY ONE
> TEACHER ONE
> BOY (point)

4. You can use objects to help your child understand how indexing is used to show one and more than one.

> For example, if your child has some plastic animals, you can place two cows in an area and three dogs in another area and sign:

> COW 2 (point 2 times to the cows)
> DOG 3 (point 1 time to your left)

> Next time try indexing (pointing) to show your child where to put the animals and let him place them in the appropriate areas.

5. Use the previous idea as a family by using little squares cut out of different pieces of colored paper. For example, you can give each person five blue squares and five red squares.

One person will give the instructions just by signing a color and indexing to show how many squares to put and where to put them. For example:

One person could sign:
BLUE (point 3 times to the right)
RED (point 2 times to the left)

Family members must use their own squares to follow the instructions. In the above example, family members would respond by putting 3 blue square to the right and 2 red squares to the left.

6. You can play a variation of the family game described above by adding other colors and instead of giving each family member his own squares, you can let each person take turns using the squares. This way you can make the game more challenging. Remember when indexing, you can use all of the space around you, not just left and right.

This game can be played using colors, shapes, or any familiar objects that can be manipulated.

7. You can also practice this new skill by asking your child to give you certain objects.

For example, set several books out on the floor and ask your child to give them to you. Practice using plurality and singularity in your requests.

BOOK (point to one) GIVE ME
BOOK (point to two specific ones) GIVE ME
BOOK 3 GIVE ME

DOLL (point to one or two) GIVE ME
CARS (use the CL: 3 to indicate how many)

8. You can practice with plurals when helping your child clean up his toys. You can point out certain objects and how many when telling your child to put them in the toy box.

BALL 3 PUT-IN BOX
GAMES (POINT) PUT-IN BOX
CARS MANY (point to them)

Lesson 26
Showing Courtesy

You can begin showing your child how to use courtesies such as thank you, please, and you're welcome.

> PLEASE
> THANK YOU
> YOU ARE WELCOME
> I AM SORRY
> EXCUSE ME

The sign PLEASE may be used at the beginning or end of the sentence.

ENGLISH	GLOSS FOR ASL
Please give me the ball.	PLEASE BALL YOU-GIVE-ME
	BALL YOU-GIVE-ME PLEASE

The sign THANK YOU is a one-sign response that is used as you would typically use thank you in English.

ENGLISH	GLOSS FOR ASL
Thank you for helping me.	YOU-HELP-ME THANK YOU
	THANK YOU HELP-ME

| PLEASE | THANK YOU | SORRY | EXCUSE ME |

The sign for YOU ARE WELCOME is a little different in ASL. There is a sign for WELCOME, but it means to welcome or invite someone. So you would not sign YOU WELCOME to mean you are welcome. Typically, after someone has signed THANK YOU, the response will be IT'S ALRIGHT or THUMB UP.

The sign SORRY is used to express remorse or wishing you had not done or said something. It is not used to pity or feel sorry for someone or to say something is sorry or no good.

The sign EXCUSE ME is used in situations where you would typically say "excuse me," such as when you interrupt someone or accidentally bump into someone.

Practice

Practice Sentences for You to Try

ENGLISH	GLOSS FOR ASL
Please pass the salt.	SALT YOU-GIVE-ME PLEASE
	-or- PLEASE YOU-GIVE-ME SALT
Thank you for sharing.	YOU SHARE THANK YOU
	-or- THANK YOU SHARE
Excuse me.	EXCUSE ME
I am sorry.	SORRY
Thank you for helping me.	YOU-HELP-ME THANK YOU
	-or- THANK YOU HELP-ME
You are welcome.	YOU'RE WELCOME (**thumb up or alright**)
Please help me clean up.	PLEASE YOU-HELP-ME CLEAN
Hand me the dishes, please.	DISHES YOU-GIVE-ME PLEASE
	-or- GIVE-ME DISHES PLEASE
Tell Sister you are sorry.	TELL/SAY SORRY

Activities

1. Playing with dolls or puppets may help to teach your child courtesies in ASL. Have one doll or puppet give something or do something nice for the other. Then let the other puppet or doll say THANK YOU. Let one puppet or doll bump into the other and say EXCUSE-ME or I'M SORRY. Sounds like you've been recruited for a role in Sesame Street, huh? What parents go through!

2. Remember to use courtesies as frequently as possible throughout the day, especially when your child does something that pleases you. That is a good time to practice THANK YOU.

3. Of course, mealtime is a good time to practice PLEASE and THANK YOU.

> JUICE YOU-GIVE-ME PLEASE
> THANK YOU
> YOU'RE WELCOME

4. Accidents happen all of the time. When you or another family member causes an accident to happen, take the opportunity to practice I'M SORRY or EXCUSE-ME. Soon your child will catch on! Remember, your child should be expected to be just as courteous as his hearing brothers and sisters.

Lesson 27
Conceptual Signing

Many words in English have several different meanings. It is important to choose the correct sign to represent the concept you want to share.

Below is a list of English words that have multiple meanings and the signs that can be used to represent these meanings. All of these are shown on the videotape of practice sentences.

MAKE

ENGLISH USAGE	APPROPRIATE SIGN
make a paper airplane	MAKE
make a friend	BECOME
	-or- MEET
make your bed	CLEAN
make up a story	INVENT/CREATE
make it on time	ARRIVE
make it in school	SUCCEED
make it happen	CAUSE
make her happy (not on video)	CAUSE
make him study	FORCE
make a decision	DECIDE
make a mistake	WRONG/MISTAKE
make enough money	EARN
make up after a fight	FRIENDS AGAIN
	-or- FORGIVE/RECONCILE

SAVE

ENGLISH USAGE	APPROPRIATE SIGN
save money	STORE/SAVE
save my life	SAFE/SAFETY

LAST

ENGLISH USAGE	APPROPRIATE SIGN
last forever	CONTINUE
last week	LAST-WEEK
last test	FINAL/LAST

GET

ENGLISH USAGE	APPROPRIATE SIGN
get there	ARRIVE
get out	LEAVE
	-or- QUIT
get up	STAND
get tired	BECOME
get it	UNDERSTAND
get a reward	GET
get ready	READY
get a chance	OPPORTUNITY
get away from	ESCAPE
get even with	REVENGE/EQUAL
go to get a job	FIND
barely get by	idiom: BARELY GET BY
That was close!	idiom: THAT WAS CLOSE!

HAVE

ENGLISH USAGE	APPROPRIATE SIGN
have a car	POSSESS/HAVE
have eaten, have done	FINISH
have to	MUST/NEED
have been living here	LIVE HERE SINCE
have worked as a teacher	PAST/BEFORE
don't have any	HAVE NOTHING (zero)

BE (the verb "to be" does not exist in ASL)

ENGLISH USAGE	APPROPRIATE SIGN
will be a doctor	BECOME
will be here	ARRIVE HERE

TAKE

ENGLISH USAGE	APPROPRIATE SIGN
take care of	SUPERVISE
take care	BE CAREFUL
	-or- THUMBS UP
take a job	ACCEPT
	-or- TAKE UP
take up a hobby	TAKE UP
take your time	SLOW
take a day off	VACATION/BREAK
take a bribe	MONEY-BRIBE ACCEPT
take your choice	SELECT/CHOOSE
can't take it	ENDURE CAN'T
	-or- FED UP

LOOK

ENGLISH USAGE	APPROPRIATE SIGN
look for my keys	SEARCH
look out!	BE CAREFUL
look at me	CLASSIFIER CL:2
take a look around	CLASSIFIER CL:2
looks good	APPEARS/SEEMS
looks the same	SEEM
	-or- FACE
look like your dad	FACE

MISS

ENGLISH USAGE	APPROPRIATE SIGN
miss class	ABSENT
miss my mom	MISS (index finger twists on chin)
miss the basket	MISS
miss the message	WENT BY ME
miss the mistake	OVERLOOK
miss the bus	LATE
	-or- MISS
miss the target	OFF THE MARK

RIGHT

ENGLISH USAGE	APPROPRIATE SIGN
right answer	CORRECT
right turn	RIGHT (R)
equal rights	ALRIGHT

RUN

ENGLISH USAGE	APPROPRIATE SIGN
run out of	ALL GONE
run up bill	INCREASE, ADD TO
run for office	COMPETE
run for exercise	RUN
run the office	MANAGE
run to town	GO
runny nose	DRIPPY NOSE
car is running	MACHINE

CALL

ENGLISH USAGE	APPROPRIATE SIGN
called me stupid	LABEL, NAME
call me on phone	CALL (1)
	-or- CALL (2)
call out	YELL
call on me	BECKON

BREAK/BROKE

ENGLISH USAGE	APPROPRIATE SIGN
the dishes broke	BREAK
I need a break	VACATION
	-or- REST
we are broke	BROKE
they broke up	DISASSOCIATE/UNATTACH
he broke out of jail	ESCAPE
break a habit	STOP

Practice
Practice Sentences for You to Try
(Not shown on video, sorry)

ENGLISH	GLOSS FOR ASL
I need to run to the store.	STORE GO NEED ME
We ran out of milk this morning.	NOW MORNING MILK ALL-GONE
We ran into Daddy at the store.	HAPPEN STORE WE SEE DADDY
Aunt Becky will take care of you tonight.	NOW NIGHT AUNT BECKY SUPERVISE YOU
We have to get up early in the morning.	TOMORROW MORNING EARLY WE CL: 2 (stand up) MUST
This is your last day at school.	NOW FINAL DAY SCHOOL FINISH
The dog got out of his pen.	DOG ESCAPED PEN (use classifiers to describe pen)
Help me look for your shoe.	YOUR SHOE HELP-ME SEARCH
Look out the window.	WINDOW LOOK (CL: 2 palm down) (point in that direction)
You look so pretty.	YOU (face) PRETTY
Do you have some gum?	YOU GUM HAVE (Q-y/n) -or- YOU HAVE GUM (Q-y/n)
Brother has the ball.	BROTHER BALL HAVE -or- BROTHER HAVE BALL
You have some ice cream.	YOU ICE CREAM HAVE -or- YOU HAVE ICE CREAM
Grandma has a cat.	GRANDMA CAT HAVE -or- GRANDMA HAVE CAT
I don't have a dog.	DOG NOT HAVE -or- NOT HAVE DOG

135

Activities

1. Focus on using conceptually accurate signs during daily routines with your child. Ask yourself, "Will the signs that I am using in this activity make my meaning perfectly clear to my child?"

2. Concentrate on thinking conceptually as you use ASL with your child. Rather that just thinking in English words or word order, thing about how it appears visually. Think of the ideas behind the words and use the conceptually appropriate signs to express those ideas.

3. In order to draw attention to conceptually appropriate signs, play a game with the family. Here's one idea:

   Someone thinks of a sentence that contains a word with multiple meanings, such as run. Family members then take turns signing the sentence, using the other, incorrect signs for RUN. Make this a silly, fun-loaded activity!

   EXAMPLE:
   Someone signs: MY NOSE IS RUNNING
   Other family members take turns signing the sentence using nonsense signs such as:

MY NOSE	RUN A RACE
MY NOSE	RUN LIKE A MACHINE

   Also, someone can think of a sentence with a multiple meaning word and fingerspell the word or sign it incorrectly. Then see who can come up with the appropriate sign.

   EXAMPLE:
   Someone signs: DADDY GOT UP, using the wrong sign for GET. The first person to sign incorrectly can make up the next sentence.

4. Put some things into a box or a sack. Give them to your child. Ask your child WHAT HAVE (Q-wh). Then help your child tell you what he or she has.

DOLL HAVE	BOOK HAVE
ROCK HAVE	PAPER HAVE
CUP HAVE	KEYS HAVE
SOCK HAVE	MIRROR HAVE
PENCIL HAVE	

5. Emphasize HAVE when you toss something back and forth between you and your child.
   BALL HAVE
   YOU BALL HAVE

Lesson 28
Fingerspelling

Fingerspelling is a natural part of ASL. Some English words do not have a specific sign that corresponds to them, so fingerspelling is used. Sometimes words are fingerspelled for ease of production or for emphasis.

You should not hesitate to fingerspell with your child, no matter how young your child may be. Deaf children, and hearing children who have deaf parents, learn to "read" fingerspelling very early. They do not actually read the letters and connect them with written words. They see the words as signs, as movements that represent concepts. Later, as they learn to read, they learn to connect the fingerspelling with the alphabet.

The important thing is that your child be exposed to the natural language of ASL that does include fingerspelling. Practice making the letters flow smoothly from one to the other. This takes practice, but you can master it! Fingerspelling should not be bouncy or segmented. Don't worry about speed. Clarity and smoothness are much more important.

You will discover that some English words do not have specific signs and fingerspelling is appropriate to use. This is especially true with some food items.

All months of the year are abbreviated and fingerspelled.

Parts of the body (toe, foot, arm, knee, back, leg, etc.) are fingerspelled or you can point to them.

Practice
Practice Sentences for You to Try

If the word has dashes between the letters, you should fingerspell it. If you know a sign for a word to be fingerspelled, that's great! Use the sign, then fingerspell it. It's okay to do both. Repeating a sign or fingerspelling a word, then signing it, is perfectly alright and is often done in ASL.

ENGLISH	GLOSS FOR ASL
I hurt my leg.	MY L-E-G HURT
Where is the car?	C-A-R WHERE (Q-wh)
I like pie.	P-I-E I LIKE
Do you want some cake?	C-A-K-E SOME YOU WANT (Q-y/n)
My pen broke.	MY P-E-N BROKE
Do you want some Jello?	YOU WANT J-E-L-L-LO (Q-y/n)
I like books.	I LIKE B-O-O-K-S
Please give me a cup.	C-U-P YOU-GIVE-ME PLEASE
Which toy do you want?	T-O-Y WANT WHICH (Q-wh)
The dog is hungry.	D-O-G HUNGRY
What time does the bus arrive?	B-U-S ARRIVE TIME (Q-wh)
I need some tape.	T-A-P-E NEED
I have to pay bills.	B-I-L-L-S PAY MUST ME

Activities

1. In daily activities use fingerspelling whenever a sign comes up with which you are not familiar. Also use fingerspelling for some of those short words; then use corresponding signs with which you are familiar or vice versa.

2. Look at pictures of your family with your child. You can use name signs, but go ahead and spell the names for your child too.

3. GAMES

END-A WORD
One person starts the game with any letter. The next person must add to it without ending the word. The next person adds another letter and so on. When you add a letter, though, you must have a word in mind that you can spell with those combinations of letters. The person next to you can challenge you and if you don't know the word, you are out. If you did have a
word in mind, the person who challenged you is out and you start a new word. It's fun and great practice!

EXAMPLE:

1st	T
2nd	TR
3rd	TRI
4th	TRIP

CATEGORIES
The group must first decide on a category such as fruit, cities, flowers, etc. The first person thinks of an object in that category. The next person's word must start with the last letter of the first word given. The next person's word must begin with the last letter of the previous word given, and so on until someone gets stuck with a letter and can't think of a word in the category that starts with that letter. No words can be used twice.

EXAMPLE:
CATEGORY: ANIMALS

1st	DOG
2nd	GOAT
3rd	TIGER
4th	R_____

Appendix A
Manual Alphabet

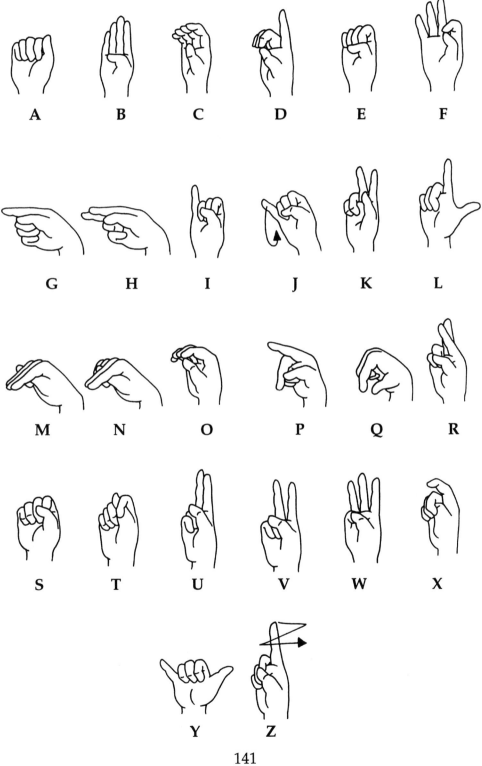

Appendix B
Numbers

Being able to express time or other measures of quantity in a meaningful, explicit manner is of vital importance. Following is a numeral system which you can easily master.

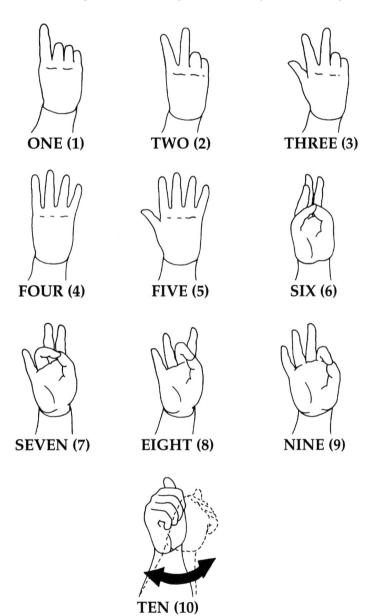

ONE (1)   **TWO (2)**   **THREE (3)**

FOUR (4)   **FIVE (5)**   **SIX (6)**

SEVEN (7)   **EIGHT (8)**   **NINE (9)**

TEN (10)

144

Appendix C
Resources

American Sign Language (The Green Books)
Charlotte Baker and Dennis Cokely
Gallaudet University Press
800 Florida Avenue NE, Washington, DC 2002-3695
202-651-5488

Signs for Me
Basic Vocabulary for Children, Parents & Teachers
Ben Bahan and Joe Dannis
DawnSignPress
9080 Activity Road, Suite A, San Diego, CA 92126
619-549-5330

The Face of ASL
MJ Bienvenu and Betty Colonomos
Sign Media, Inc.
4020 Blackburn Lane, Burtonsville, MD 20866
301-421-0268

American Sign Language Phrase Book
Lou Fant
Sign Media, Inc.
4020 Blackburn Lane, Burtonsville, MD 20866
301-421-0268

A Basic Course in American Sign Language
Tom Humphries, Carol Padden, Terrence J. O'Rourke
Copyright 1980, 1994, T.J. Publishers, Inc.
817 Silver Spring Avenue, Suite 206, Silver Spring, MD 20910
301-585-4440

Joy of Signing, 2nd Edition
Lottie L. Riekehof
Gospel Publishing House
1445 Boonville Avenue, Springfield, MO 65802

Beginning American Sign Language VideoCourse
Award Winning Series
with Billy Seago and the Bravo Family
Sign Enhancers,Inc.
1535 State Street, Salem, OR 97301
503-370-9721

Signing Naturally
(designed for use with an instructor)
Cheri Smith, Ella Mae Lentz, and Ken Mikos
DawnSignPress
9080 Activity Road, Suite A, San Diego, CA 92126
619-549-5330

American Sign Language: A Comprehensive Dictionary
Martin L.A. Sternberg, EdD
HarperCollins, Publishers, Inc.
New York, NY

The Book of Name Signs
Naming in American Sign Language
Samuel J. Supalla, PhD
DawnSignPress
9080 Activity Road, Suite A, San Diego, CA 92126
619-549-5330

148